Help Preserve Your Wealth and Leave A Legacy

IRA and Retirement Strategies
for Those with a Net Worth of
$1,000,000 to $10 Million or More

Fourth Edition: Updated July 2023

Craig Kirsner, MBA, President
Kirsner Wealth Management

Craig Kirsner, MBA/Kirsner Wealth Management
5350 West Hillsboro Blvd., Suite 103
Coconut Creek, Florida 33073
KirsnerWealth.com

Book layout ©2023 Advisors Excel, LLC

Help Preserve Your Wealth and Leave A Legacy/Craig Kirsner, MBA.
— 4th ed.

ISBN 9798771888422

To my father, Stuart Kirsner, the greatest mentor and dad a guy could ask for!

To my wife, Karen, my best supporter and an amazing wife and mother to our kids. You're the best! I love you!

To David and Cody creators of Advisors Excel... thank you for creating the best "back office" support team ever!

To my great clients, some of whom I have had the pleasure of working with for decades.

And to God for giving me the talent to help people.

I am truly blessed!

Table of Contents

Introduction by Stuart Kirsner 1

Introduction by Craig Kirsner and Sean Burke 13

Help Protect the Assets You Leave Your Family............ 31

Outright Distribution Estate Plans — A Major Potential Problem 35

"Per Stirpes" Doesn't Necessarily Keep Your Assets in Your Family Bloodline 37

Divorce and Lawsuits: Major Potential Destroyers of Your Wealth 39

Having the Right Estate Plan Is Very Important to Help Protect Your Assets After You're Gone 43

One Solution: The Dynasty Revocable Trust................. 45

Protect Your Grandchildren.. 51

State Estate and Income Taxes 55

The Importance of Beneficiary Designations 57

How to Fund Your Living Trust 61

You Can Leave Your IRA to Your Trust 63

Revocable Versus Irrevocable Trusts........................... 67

What's the Downside to a Dynasty Revocable Trust?.... 69

Wills 71

Specific Gifts to Loved Ones.. 75

Other Vital Estate Planning Documents: Powers of Attorney 77

Memorial Instructions 81

A Survivor's Checklist 83

Estate Taxes and Income Taxes 87

Warren Buffett's Rules of Investing 93

Why Use a Financial Professional? 107

What Does Our 3 Bucket Retirement Financial Plan Look Like? 115

Investment Strategies for the Different Stages of the Economic Cycle 125

What Is Tactical Investing? 129

Can Risk Management Saves Lives? 133

Seven Golden Rules for Investing and Advanced Estate Planning 137

Financial Concerns for a Surviving Spouse 143

The Myth That You Should Always be Fully Invested in the Market 155

Special Report: Are Blue-Chip, Dividend-Paying Stocks Really "Safe?" 159

7 Myths About Variable Annuities: Exposing Their Dark Side 165

Income Taxes and the "Elimination" of the Stretch IRA 177

You Should Have a Personal Umbrella Liability Insurance Policy 191

What is Cryptocurrency and Blockchain? 193

How Might Archegos' $10 Billion in Losses Affect Your Retirement? 207

Longevity 207

Retirement Income 221

Annuities 235

How to Save Money on Your Life Insurance 243

Social Security 251

The Kirsner Wealth Management Team 267

Best and Worst Days of the Stock Market 269

Biographies 273

Featured Appearances 283

Introduction by Stuart Kirsner, Retired founder of our company

Stuart Kirsner, Founder of Stuart Estate Planning in 1972, with more than 46 years' experience as a licensed insurance agent

The following is a photo of my dad when he was eight years old, fishing in Prospect Park in Brooklyn, New York. He enjoyed a young boy's typical, worry-free life back then. He lived in a one-bedroom apartment in a nice neighborhood in Bensonhurst, Brooklyn. His brother and him slept on a pullout couch in the living room, which was covered in the most uncomfortable "protective plastic covering" to keep the couch clean and your butt sweaty when you sat on it. My dad's dad didn't make very much money but earned enough so that all his needs were taken care of.

My dad was a partner in a 30-year-old auto parts business in Brooklyn. He was the outside salesman and his business partner handled all the finances, banking and inventory. Soon after the picture above was taken, his business partner had a heart attack and died.

My dad did the best he could to take over the whole business but the truth was that his dad didn't even attend high school and didn't know the first thing about math or finances. So, not very long after that the business failed and sadly, soon after that his dad had a heart attack and died... The stress was just too great for him.

His dad left my dad a meager bank account and his family struggled for many years after that. That experience caused me to swear as a young man that he would never leave his family with the kind of financial mess that his Dad left him in. He swore to learn everything he could about money, business, finances, investments, real estate, and insurance, so his family would never have to suffer like we did when he was young.

That lesson served him well. We have learned that we have to take great care of client's financial needs as our firm has done for decades, even since I retired in 2017. Our goal is to produce solid satisfaction and happiness for our clients, which leads to continued successful results for our business. Now I don't know if you grew up with financial struggles like he did, however I'm sure you've had your share of trials and tribulations in life like we have all had, so for over fifty years we've helped families just like you who are looking to help preserve their wealth, minimize taxes and keep their money with their family after they're gone and that's what we're going to talk about in this book.

In the 1970s and 1980s, my dad built a large, very successful, retirement, estate, and insurance business in New York City. He had 88 employees in midtown Manhattan. My son Craig grew up around my business. He's had his insurance license since he was 18 years old.

Our family moved to South Florida from New York City in 1987 and dad continued his retirement and estate services business. He didn't have any connections in South Florida so he decided to experiment with public-invited, advanced estate and retirement dinner seminars for families with estates greater than $3 million dollars in value. Seminars were a costly investment. They were held at very fancy local restaurants. He took out expensive, full-page ads in all the local newspapers advertising the seminars. All the critics told him that he was crazy to do that, that no people who were truly rich would show up to a public-invited estate seminar. He proved all his critics wrong... very wrong. Having only thirty seats in the Dinner Seminar room, He actually had over 500 people show up for the first seminar. So many that he actually had to turn most of the people away and set up many more seminars for the overflow of guests alone! This was the start of an amazing business journey.

Since then, the business journey continues. We've made a wonderful name for ourselves in South Florida. We've continued this successful estate and retirement seminar tradition at Ruth's Chris and Abe & Louie's Restaurant. And now many other advisors have attempted to copy our dinner seminar formula. And thankfully, seminar attendees consistently tell us that our seminar was the best, by far, they've ever attended.

He's very proud of his son Craig's accomplishments to date, and in this particularly insightful retirement planning book, my son shares the insights he has gained working side-by-side with me in the estate and retirement services business. With decades of service, we've worked with many retirees to help them achieve financial confidence. I was one of the early pioneers in the estate and retirement income industry, I've helped many families during my 46 years in the insurance business.

Today, people have real worries about running out of money in their retirement years. Craig will show you ways to help avoid that by using a few strategies for potentially squeezing higher payments from assets like your Social Security account (find some "hidden" values there), your pension (monthly income or lump sum?), your nest egg savings (how much risk is too much? Should you buy an annuity to help preserve your principal?), and your retirement accounts (exactly how to invest these assets and — critically — how much to withdraw from your savings each year). The right moves might be able to raise the amount you have to spend, and they could stretch out your money over many more years.

Craig will help you identify potentially costly retirement planning mistakes, which are all too common. Just because you added to your 401(k) or IRA plan every year, invested wisely, and amassed significant savings, you are not necessarily home free. Every day, people just like you, people who have worked hard and saved carefully for retirement, make unwise decisions that could ultimately crack their retirement nest egg. This is all avoidable with sensible planning.

You'll learn how to help safeguard your hard-earned retirement assets, because, contrary to what most people think, it is not necessarily poor portfolio performance that often busts your retirement accounts. It might be the emotional decisions you make that can have an enormous impact on your ability to continue to enjoy a comfortable retirement and financial peace of mind.

Craig will explain how to address the risks to lifetime financial security, such as longer life expectancy, potentially excessive risk in your portfolio, excessive fees, low investment returns, high taxes, and more. You'll learn how to plan for the wildcards of retirement planning: increasing health care and long-term care expenses.

This book covers important changes in key retirement areas such as IRA management, tactical investing, estate planning, annuities, and income taxes. You'll learn ways to merge these insights into your own financial plan to help you enhance your financial security, and ability to provide for loved ones in the future.

Retirement no longer means being put out to pasture. Today's retirees are traveling the world, attending classes, developing new skills, starting businesses, mastering neglected hobbies, and more. They do this well into their golden years. This guide helps you work towards the financial independence to pursue the retirement you want through smart planning and effective financial strategies.

You'll learn ways to help:
- Turn your retirement savings into lifetime income you and your spouse cannot outlive
- Avoid some common and costly risks to a retiree's financial security
- Determine how much risk you should you have now
- Understand the right way to develop a sustainable spending strategy
- Minimize taxes in retirement
- Invest your retirement portfolio with the goal of making it last as long as you do, and then leave a legacy for loved ones

Above all, you'll learn about ways to help make your retirement years the best time of your life.

Craig offers a great deal of retirement wisdom and many of his best, most successful, time-tested retirement planning tools and strategies. The goal is to help you achieve a satisfying and successful retirement.

We look at your wealth like a coin that has two sides: one side is to make sure you have a diversified retirement plan to help ensure you have enough money to last for the rest of you and your spouse's lives. And the back side of the coin is your legacy because most of our clients have children and grandchildren that they love. That's why most of these people, regardless of the size of their estates, usually want the same thing. They want to avoid the expensive costs of probate after they're gone, they want to minimize the taxes on their estate at death, they want to the whole process to be simple and quick and private for their children, without the need for expensive lawyers and accountants, and they want to make sure that the assets they leave to their children after they die will never pass to spouses of their children through a messy divorce or through the death of one of their children. This is exactly what attorney Jack Owen, Esquire, CPA, will discuss in Section 1 of this book. I'm not an attorney, however the following are some stories of what I've seen over the past forty-six years in this business.

I'm reminded of a person we met at a seminar — we'll call him Smith Junior — who came to one of our estate planning seminars and then met with us who was quite angry. He shared that his dad, Smith Senior, who died over two years ago, had an attorney who didn't "believe" in the need for trusts. The attorney had told his dad, Smith Senior, that the use of a will was the simplest and easiest way to leave his estate to his children.

Well, we well know that a will is a ticket to the probate courts. We say "courts" in plural because if a client owns assets in different states, as his dad, Smith Senior, did, those assets have to go through the probate process in each of the states they are owned in. For Smith Junior, he had to probate Smith Senior's assets throughout multiple states and their various processes and established laws. Because the clients had a so-called "simple-will" type estate plan, Smith Junior had to deal with over two years of long unnecessary delays, wasted time and energy, very high legal and accounting fees, far higher estate taxes than were necessary and tons of correspondence merely to establish the fact that his dad had legal title to all the assets he was leaving to his children.

Smith Junior had come to one of our estate planning seminars and listened to the attorney presenting there learned very clearly that by correctly using a modern revocable living trust, he and his wife after they're gone could avoid the entire probate process completely and leave their assets quickly and inexpensively to their children and grandchildren.

The advanced estate planning attorneys we partner with worked with them to set up their dynasty revocable living trust which included all the details of what they wanted regarding who got what and when and how after they were both gone. They also set up specific provisions as to how the assets would be used for one of their grandchildren, who had special needs.

As is common, Smith Junior and his wife were named trustees of their revocable trust which meant that they were in control of all the assets in the trust during their entire lifetime. They included disability provisions and named who would control the trust in the event they couldn't. The living trust provisions were changeable at any time and the entire trust itself was completely revocable at any time. After Smith Junior had all the provisions and language in the trust that they wanted, they simply transferred all their assets, without any taxes payable when moved into the trust. Income and other taxes may be due on some assets, but putting those assets into the trust would not trigger an automatic tax, and could prevent additional estate taxes.

Now, he was very happy knowing that regardless of which spouse dies first, the probate process could be completely avoided. Now, there would be no long delays and expensive legal accounting fees. Now, both Smith Junior and his wife's estate tax-free exemptions would be planned for saving as much as thousands in taxes. Now, after his wife and he were gone, Smith Junior took comfort in knowing that his son-in-law, whom he had no respect for, would never get a penny of the money he left to his daughter.

Needless to say, Smith Junior was thrilled with what our attorneys had done for him, especially knowing that their children would not have to go through the years of pain that he had to go through in settling his dad's estate.

What's fascinating, and not commonly known, is that for a very long time, this kind of so-called dynasty revocable living trust planning was only utilized by the few who could afford to use a fairly small group of savvy and expensive professional attorneys and accountants and planners who worked in this specialized field.

If, for example, you had a Rockefeller-sized estate that would be hit with a 40% estate tax on everything you owned after you and your spouse died, due in cash within nine months after the death of the second spouse, beyond the estate tax free exemption, that might not be a problem, these professionals might say. They'd likely suggest using use a combination of "special" trusts and strategies that were available then to help minimize or eliminate all estate taxes that might be owed.

For example, they might use a combination of an Irrevocable Dynasty Trust, a Family Limited Partnership, and a Personal Residence Trust to potentially eliminate all of the estate taxes owed by an ultra-wealthy estate at death. Using a combination of these strategies, there might not be much left in your estate to tax, and then the trust assets could pass tax-free to whoever you choose.[1]

Oh yes, and these assets while you're alive could be lawsuit and creditor protected. And yes, the trust could also help to ensure that the assets you leave to your children and grandchildren are forever protected in the event your children ever get divorced, protected if your children ever get sued, protected if your children intentionally or unintentionally wanted to leave the trust assets to a non family member, and, by the way, could be protected from the second 40% estate tax levied on the

---

[1] Robert A. Ross and Stacy A. Vogeltanz. Ross Estate Planning. "Advanced Estate Planning Topics."
https://rossestateplanning.com/global_pictures/Advanced_Estate_Planning_Topics.pdf https://rossestateplanning.com/practice-area/estate-planning/

trust assets that are left after your children are gone that pass to their children, your grandchildren.

Alternatively, for those who wanted to keep their estate tax planning simple and were just concerned with avoiding the impact of the 40% estate tax levied on all their estate assets at death, the professional might instead recommend a "special" irrevocable trust and have you purchase a life insurance policy with a face amount that would cover all the estate taxes on your estate at death, assuming you could qualify medically. The trust would be set up so the premiums you'd pay, on which you've paid income taxes already, would be estate and gift tax free.

Over these many years, estate planning laws have changed and the taxes on estates now apply mostly to the very rich since the estate tax exemption has been greatly increased.

Today people often come to our team to request that the attorney establish an estate plan for them with the same types of benefits and protections that the Rockefeller family enjoyed.

Surprisingly, not much has changed in what clients come to us for. Again, regardless of the size of the estate, more than anything these clients have wanted to accomplish in the estate planning process our team would do for them, would be to make sure that "daughter-in-law" of mine, or "that son in law" of mine doesn't get a penny of mine after my wife and I are gone.

What goes around ... comes around ...

Stuart Kirsner,
Founder of Stuart Estate Planning
Stuart Kirsner is not affiliated with Kirsner Wealth Management or AEWM.

Section 1:

Dynasty Estate Planning Strategies for Millionaires: Help Keep The Assets You Leave Your Children Protected from Potential Future Divorces, Lawsuits, and Creditor Claims; and Help Ensure Your Assets Stay In Your Family Bloodline

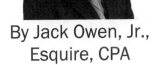

By Jack Owen, Jr.,
Esquire, CPA

Grandchildren!

Introduction by Retirement Planning Professional, Investment Advisor Representative, Author and Speaker, Craig Kirsner, MBA, President, and Sean Burke, M.S., Vice President of Kirsner Wealth Management

W hy do you do estate planning? For most people, the answer is that they love their grandchildren!

My dad, Stuart Kirsner, always says he should have had grandchildren first... You play with them for a few hours, you get tired, and you give them back! What's better than that?

Kirsner Wealth Management has a strategic partnership with tax professionals and attorneys who can provide tax and/or legal advice. Neither Kirsner Wealth Management or its representatives may give legal or tax advice. You are encouraged to consult your tax advisor or attorney. Jack Owen, Jr. Esquire, is not affiliated with Kirsner Wealth Management or AEWM.

For most of my retired millionaire clients ages sixty-five to eighty-five, they typically want to do estate planning so the money they worked so hard to accumulate will one day go to their grandchildren after their children pass away — they will help stay in their family bloodline.

My clients might take or leave their children on certain days, but they always love their grandchildren!

A properly designed dynasty revocable living trust is designed to help protect the assets you leave your children and grandchildren from any future divorces, lawsuits, and creditor claims. The dynasty revocable living trust also helps keep your assets in your family bloodline ... so after you're gone your assets can't go to your ex-son-in-law, they will only go to your children and then to your grandchildren ... they will stay in your family bloodline.

I'm Sean Burke, M.S., Vice President and Director of Insitutional Money Management at Kirsner Wealth Management. Previously, I was a financial advisor at Fidelity helping people plan for their retirement. I help Kirsner Wealth Management Wealth Advisor's clients establish plans and strategies that help to achieve their financial goals. These conversations include tax-efficient investing, investment strategy with proper risk management, estate planning, principal and income protection, and more.

To educate our clients, we have been doing dinner seminars at the Ruth's Chris steakhouse for over thirty years here in the Boca Raton area and all over the country.

The following are the estate planning slides taken directly from our dinner seminar that describe some of the problems we see regarding advanced estate planning and some of the solutions the attorneys we work with make available to our clients. The first section of slides are my introductory slides and then Jack Owen, Esquire, does his slides as shown:

One of the attorneys we've worked with for decades is here tonight, Jack Owen, who is an advanced estate planning attorney and a CPA.

Jack specializes in setting up trusts that are designed to help protect the assets you leave to your children and grandchildren from any future divorces, lawsuits and creditor claims. His trusts are designed to keep your assets in your family bloodline.

Many people want this type of dynasty estate plan; however, as Jack will discuss, you probably don't have this type of plan.

Jack Owen can help improve
the quality of your estate plan,
because planning your estate can
be difficult. Many people often have
complicated family circumstances.
He, along with our team, can help make it
easier for you to properly put the plan in
place that meets your goals and needs.

There are people in this room
with a daughter-in-law or
a son-in-law they just don't like.
(I've heard that many, many times!)

Jack Owen can help with an estate plan
that's designed so that the assets you
leave your children don't go to
that daughter-in-law or son-in-law
after you're gone.

There are people in this room who have a child who is a spendthrift or an alcoholic or an addict. The trust that Jack Owen sets up can help protect those children.

The majority of our clients want their assets go to their grandchildren after their children pass away.

The trust that Jack Owen sets up can help keep the assets in your family bloodline

I am now very pleased
to introduce Attorney
Jack Owen, Esquire, CPA

We have worked
with Jack for decades and
he focuses on advanced estate planning.
Jack earned his law degree from the
University of Florida and graduated
in the top 10% of his class.

Jack has been a practicing attorney
since 1985 and a CPA since 1981.
He owns his own law firm in
Palm Beach, Florida.

A <u>will</u> is a simple way to leave your assets to your Beneficiaries after you're gone, but the fact is...

*Your estate <u>WILL</u> go to probate;

*There is public disclosure of your assets, debts and heirs;

*Probate is expensive and time-consuming.

In Florida, a probate case can take up to 2 years to complete and the legal fees could cost up to 5% of the value of your estate![2]

---

[2] NOLO. Mary Randolph. Accessed March 1, 2023. "Florida Probatee: An Overview." https://www.nolo.com/legal-encyclopedia/florida-probatean-overview.html

A **revocable living trust** is also a simple way to leave your assets to your beneficiaries after you're gone, AND...

*No probate;

*No public disclosure of your assets, debt and heirs;

*No delay in distribution

You can pass your assets by beneficiary designation...

The good news is that this avoids probate

The bad news is those assets will not be protected from potential lawsuits and divorce.

And they won't be bloodline protected.

Unfortunately, about 90% of all wills and living trust estate plans that Jack Owen has reviewed over the past 38 years wind up being nothing more than

OUTRIGHT DISTRIBUTION ESTATE PLANS

IF YOU DO HAVE AN
OUTRIGHT DISTRIBUTION WILL
or REVOCABLE LIVING TRUST

The assets you leave your children,
including your I.R.A.,
will be completely exposed to:

LOSS in the event of a child's divorce

LOSS from passing directly to a son-in-law or a daughter-in-law, at your child's death

LOSS from passing to a grandchild at too young of an age

Many trusts do have language in them that set up divorce protection and bloodline-protected trusts for your children after you're gone...

However, many also say to distribute:

1/3 of the trust to your children at <u>age 25</u>

1/2 when they reach <u>age 30</u>

and the balance to them at <u>age 35</u>

It's possible that your children will be older than age 35 when you die.

That's why we feel that many plans wind up being

Outright Distribution Plans...
<u>With Little Protection</u>

**Many clients believe that
because their estate plan has
Per Stirpes language in it, that...**

**This will help protect the assets
and keep them in the bloodline
after they're gone ... It won't**

And it could create unexpected problems
for your grandchildren. **Here's why**...

**If your son is NOT living
at the time of your death,
Per Stirpes provisions will pass the
assets you left him down to his children**

However, the problem is...they'll
go directly to his children when the children
become the age of majority, which is age 18
or 21 in most states, regardless of the amount.

**We believe that distributing assets
to an 18 year old is a bit too young.
Wouldn't you agree?**

But... the more likely scenario is that your son is alive at the time of your death and has received the assets you left him...

and then he dies <u>anytime</u> after that

The assets you left him will then pass by way of his will or his trust, if he has one... or by state law if he has no plan...

to his wife... your daughter-in-law.

Completely avoidable with proper planning

If your daughter, for example, gets divorced after receiving the assets you left her,

all the assets you left her

plus all the assets she accumulated during the marriage to your soon to be ex-son-in-law...

could be completely <u>exposed to loss</u> in a messy divorce.

As part of your complimentary consultation with our team, you'll learn exactly how a <u>Dynasty Revocable Living Trust</u>,
with multi-generation provisions can help protect the assets you leave your children and your grandchildren,
including your IRA.

Protected from future divorces, lawsuits or creditors
and your children, if so elected, will be in complete control over the trust assets you leave them and the income from the trust.

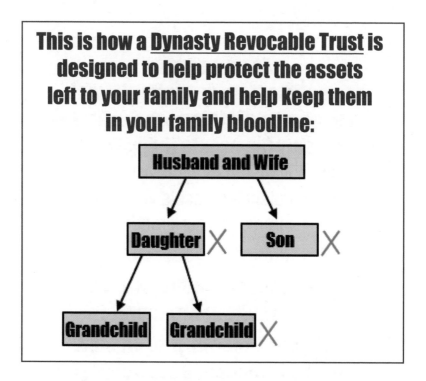

To briefly summarize how a dynasty revocable trust is designed to work as shown in the example above, the assets are for the husband and wife while they are alive. There is no change while you're alive as the trust is revocable, or changeable at any time.

After both the husband and wife die, the assets are split 50% to your daughter and 50% to your son. Your children can control all of the assets in each of their individual trusts, if that's what you want.

The assets you leave your children are kept in asset-protected trusts that are designed to help protect your heirs from potential future divorces, lawsuits and creditor claims.

The trust assets are also designed to be bloodline protected. So when your daughter dies, the assets that are in her special trust doesn't go to her spouse, they only go down to your grandchildren in asset-protected trusts for your grandchildren's benefit.

Lastly, if your son doesn't have children when he dies, then his trust assets will only go to your daughter or her children to help keep your assets in your family bloodline.

This is what the vast majority of our millionaire clients want, but unfortunately nine times out of ten, this is not what the client's plans that I review actually have in them.

> **If your estate size is more than $12.9 million for an individual, or $25.8 million for a couple, your family could have an estate tax situation at your death, <u>so we have special estate tax savings strategies to discuss with you.</u>[3]**

---

[3] IRS.gov. January 2023. "What's New-Estate and Gift Tax." https://www.irs.gov/businesses/small-businesses-self-employed/whats-new-estate-and-gift-tax

And for those <u>charitably inclined</u>,
we can discuss charitable planning tools
that might allow you to sell
highly appreciated assets today
and pay no capital gains tax.
You may qualify to receive
a tax deduction now as well.

And you may get income
for the rest of your life from that trust.[4]

Then, when you die, the balance of
those assets left in the trust go to the
charity or charities of your choice.

---

[4] IRS, Accessed March 2, 2023 "Charitable Remainder Trusts", https://www.irs.gov/charities-non-profits/charitable-remainder-trusts

Clients of Jack Owen receive credit card shaped USB cards to carry in your wallet that have copies of all your legal documents on them,

so you can carry your important documents everywhere, and give additional copies to your children.

A sample USB card is shown below:

RETIRE STRONG
Estate Planning Documents
Craig Kirsner, MBA, President

In real life, this is the size of a <u>credit card</u>, where we put PDF copies of your signed legal documents on the flash drive shown above.

Help Protect the Assets You Leave Your Family

By Jack Owen, Jr., Esquire, CPA
Estate Planning Attorney and CPA

Many of my clients are retired millionaires and they want to protect the assets they've worked so hard to accumulate. They want to pass on their assets to their children and grandchildren, so they need a modern estate plan designed to help protect these assets from potential future divorces, lawsuits, and creditor claims.

Something that is often very important to them is ensuring their assets stay in their family bloodline — they want their assets to go to their grandchildren after their children pass away, not their child's spouse. We call those people "out-laws!" This type of trust planning isn't just for millionaires, I believe if your estate is over $500,000 in value, then it's worth protecting with proper estate planning documents.

I have been a practicing attorney since 1985 and a CPA since 1981. I earned my law degree from the University of Florida, where I graduated with honors in the top 10% of my class. I own my own law firm, where a majority of my practice concentrates on advanced estate planning matters and real estate matters.

It's very important to my clients that their legacy is secured with proper estate planning documents. And I am very pleased to have worked with Stuart and Craig Kirsner of Kirsner Wealth Management for over twenty-five years.

In my practice, I have seen a lot of mistakes in estate planning. Clients, or clients' families, have come in after a death in the family and have found themselves in the middle of probate or high taxes. They might have discovered that something unforeseen (such as long-term care) drained the estate. I've seen inheritances lost due to divorces, lawsuits, or even improper beneficiary designations.

Although there are many people who suffer from a loved one's failure to plan, I have also had many clients who have family members who left rich legacies. These clients might be grieving their loved one's loss, but at the same time, their relief is inexpressible. The knowledge that their loved one was looking out for them in both life and death is one of the greatest gifts they could receive.

A Jack Owen Client Story:

One of my clients died and he left his daughter money in a dynasty trust that I set up.

His daughter was driving in Palm Beach County and unfortunately changed lanes without seeing a motorcyclist, who crashed and lost his leg.

The personal injury attorneys that motorcyclist hired poured over the trust using specialists looking for any way they could to pierce the trust and get their hands on the trust assets. Thankfully, they couldn't do so. The trust did what it was supposed to do — it protected my client's daughter from lawsuits and creditor claims.

Fortunately, my client's daughter had a $1 million umbrella liability coverage policy, so the attorneys went after that when they realized they couldn't take money out of the trust I set up for her benefit and protection.

The above is an example of proper estate planning where the daughter's inherited assets were free from her creditor's claims.

This is an example provided for illustrative purposes only; it should not be construed as advice designed to meet the particular needs of an individual's situation.

CHAPTER ONE

Outright Distribution Estate Plans — A Major Potential Problem

A major problem I see in my estate planning practice is that roughly 90% of all the wills or revocable trusts I review have "outright distribution" language in them. If you have an outright distribution will or revocable living trust, the assets you leave to your children, including your IRA, could be completely exposed to:

- Loss in the event of a child's divorce
- Loss in the event of a lawsuit against your child
- Loss from passing directly to a son-in-law or a daughter-in-law at your child's death
- Loss from passing to a grandchild at too young of an age

Many trusts do have language in them that set up divorce-protected and bloodline-protected trusts for your children after you're gone. However, many trusts and wills also say to distribute:

- One-third of the trust to your children at age 25,
- One-half when they reach age 30,
- and the balance to them at age 35.

The trouble with this is that most of my client's children will be older than age 35 when they die. That's why most plans wind up being outright distribution plans with little protection.

So if you keep your children's money in trust rather than outright distribute the money to them upon your death or at certain ages, then the money retains the creditor and bloodline protections of the trust.

Another example in what I see my client's children do with outright distributions of inherited assets is buy a new home that is usually titled in joint names with that child's spouse. The new home is now a joint asset subject to being split 50-50 with your child's spouse in the event of a divorce. Unfortunately, we are seeing our clients' children getting divorced even after many years of marriage.

CHAPTER TWO

"Per Stirpes" Doesn't Necessarily Keep Your Assets in Your Family Bloodline

Many clients believe that, because their estate plan has "per stirpes" language in it, that this will protect the assets and keep them in the bloodline after they're gone. It might not. And it could create unexpected problems for your grandchildren. Here's why:

Yes, if your son is not living at the time of your death, per stirpes provisions will pass the assets you left him down to his children. However, the problem is that the assets could go directly to his children when the children become the "age of majority," which is age eighteen or twenty-one in most states, regardless of the amount. Generally, we believe distributing assets to an eighteen-year-old is a bit too young. Wouldn't you agree?

However, the more likely scenario is that your son is alive at the time of your death and he receives the assets you left him. Then, he dies any time after that, whether it's

37

the next day or twenty years later. The assets you left him will then pass by way of his will or his trust if he has one, or by state law if he has no plan, to his wife, your daughter-in-law.

What happens if your ex-daughter-in-law then gets married to someone who already has children? If she dies and leaves that money to her new husband, do you think the money he inherits will go to his children, or your grandchildren? In my experience, most of the time it goes to the former, out of the bloodline. This is not what my clients want and it's completely avoidable with proper planning.

CHAPTER THREE

Divorce and Lawsuits: Major Potential Destroyers of Your Wealth

If your daughter, for example, gets divorced after receiving the assets you left her, all the assets you left her, as well as all the assets she accumulated during the marriage to your soon-to-be ex-son-in-law, could be completely exposed to loss in a messy divorce. With a 40 to 50% divorce rate in America, it's very important to protect the assets you leave your children and grandchildren from divorce.[5]

Now, you might have been told that if you leave assets directly to your daughter and she keeps those assets separate from her husband, it will protect her if she got divorced. While that may be true, what I have seen in my practice is that your daughter loves her husband and the assets get comingled together. At this point, they become a marital asset.

---

[5] Wilkinson & Finkbeiner Family Law Attorneys. 2022. "Divorce Statistics: Over 115 Studies, Facts and Rates for 2022." https://www.wf-lawyers.com/divorce-statistics-and-facts/

Why take a chance when this is completely avoidable with a proper plan? My mother always said to hope for the best but plan for the worst.

Lawsuits: Another Major Potential Destroyer of Your Wealth

We live in a very litigious society. And the more assets you have, the more of a target you become.

A Jack Owen Client Story:

Potential lawsuits include divorce, personal injury, business disputes, and personal disputes. I have seen my clients' children involved in foreclosures and accusations of wrong-doing in business and personal disputes. Therefore, keeping the assets you leave to your children in a trust protects those assets from your children's litigation creditors.

I always recommend to my clients to get an umbrella liability policy through their homeowners or auto insurance when appropriate, which could protect their assets should a lawsuit happen.

For only about $500 per year (the cost obviously varies by state and insurer), you can buy a $1 million liability policy, which often makes a lot of sense. I typically recommend having enough liability coverage to cover the value of your assets, with a minimum of $1 million. It's usually quite affordable, so why not?

Also, if a lawsuit occurs, in my experience, they just go after the deep pockets of the insurance company and try to settle with them out of court as quickly as possible, which is why I believe an umbrella policy can be a smart decision.

This is an example provided for illustrative purposes only; it should not be construed as advice designed to meet the particular needs of an individual's situation.

CHAPTER FOUR

Having the Right Estate Plan Is Very Important to Help Protect Your Assets After You're Gone

Y ou have no reason to skip out on your legacy and estate planning. People often put off setting up an estate plan for years or even decades.

Without a proper estate plan, your estate could be tied up in the probate court, which could take over a year to complete and cost up to 8% of your estate's value in legal fees.[6] Probate attorneys are quite expensive, so you want to avoid this process by setting up your estate properly while you're alive.

What might be worse is if you are someday unable to make decisions for yourself in your old age. As far as I'm concerned, planning for the worst is one of the best ways to show your love. So show it and avoid expensive potential legal fees.

---

[6] LegalMatch. Oct. 27, 2020. "The Cost of Probate: A State Comparison." https://www.legalmatch.com/law-library/article/the-cost-of-probate-a-state-comparison.html

Also, probate can become a public matter. Certain probate matters are available for review by the public. We have seen in recent years many famous people such as the author Tom Clancy or entertainers Aretha Franklin and Prince die without proper estate planning where their assets, beneficiaries and other personal matters are exposed for public consumption.

On the other hand, assets received by way of your trust are not exposed to the public in regards to how much and what type of assets are being inherited. This trust privacy can be important for your children.

I have had several of my client's children tell me that, after their parents' probate, several charities approached them for either new or increased contributions because the charities learned the children had inherited assets from the public probate records. One child said his children's private school wanted increased donations because of the inheritance from the parents. Don't underestimate the fact that confidentiality could help your loved ones.[7]

---

[7] Kirsner Wealth Management has a strategic partnership with tax professionals and attorneys who can provide tax and/or legal advice. Neither Kirsner Wealth Management or its representatives may give legal or tax advice. You are encouraged to consult your tax advisor or attorney. Jack Owen, Jr. Esquire, is not affiliated with Kirsner Wealth Management or AEWM.

CHAPTER FIVE

One Solution: The Dynasty Revocable Trust

One of the most important tools of legacy planning, in my opinion, is the dynasty revocable living trust. A dynasty trust with multi-generation provisions is designed to protect the assets you leave to your children and your grandchildren, including your IRA. It is designed to be protected from any future divorces, lawsuits, or creditor claims. And it helps ensure that your assets stay in your family bloodline for many generations. We call these "dynasty" trusts because the trust can last several generations and because of the asset and bloodline protection features they include.

The dynasty trust is revocable, which means it is completely changeable at any time while you're alive. Your wishes become irrevocable and unchangeable upon your death which his when your assets go to your heirs in trust.

The dynasty revocable living trust is the workhorse of your estate plan. It organizes and simplifies your estate, so that if you ever become disabled, or when you die, the estate administration costs and delays are minimized. You always determine who gets what, when and how and under what circumstances, and you may change any of the provisions of your trust at any time. You are typically the trustee of your own trust while you're alive and capable and have complete control over the trust assets during your lifetime.

It is very important that once the trust is created that the majority of your assets, outside of your IRA, should all be retitled tax-neutrally into your trust. This is important and will be addressed later. The tax ID number of your trust while you're alive is your Social Security number, so there will be no change at all in your tax situation.

The Dynasty Trust Avoids Probate

If you can, you want to avoid probate at all costs! Stu Kirsner always said that lawyers write very slowly at $450 an hour when they are probating your estate!

Probate means to prove who you want to leave your assets to.[8] Using proper trust planning should eliminate the long administrative delays and often high legal fees estates might have to deal with at the time a person dies. All the assets that are titled in your trust at your death, no matter where in the U.S. the asset happens to be, should avoid the costs and delays of the probate system.

Unfortunately, some of my clients do not properly retitle all of their assets to be in the name of their trust. When this happens, then it becomes necessary to have a "mini" probate for those assets not titled in the trust name at the client's death. Assets to look out for that definitely need to be retitled are real estate and all bank accounts.

---

[8] LegalMatch. Oct. 27, 2020. "The Cost of Probate: A State Comparison." https://www.legalmatch.com/law-library/article/the-cost-of-probate-a-state-comparison.html

A Jack Owen Client Story:

I see clients forget to retitle into their trust an out-of-state vacation home. So when this happens, assuming a jointly titled asset, then upon the second to die between the husband and wife, a probate has to be opened in Florida and then an ancillary probate has to be opened in the state where the vacation home is located. Two probates!

Again, this can be avoided by re-titling the vacation home in the name of the client's trust.

We will discuss the pitfalls of probate and the fact that a will is a ticket to the probate court a little later in this book.

What Happens When You Die With a Dynasty Trust

If you are married at the time of your death, then at the first spouse's death, typically the surviving spouse becomes the primary beneficiary and controlling trustee over all the assets the deceased spouse owned.

The surviving spouse has complete control over all the assets in the trust and can get all the income needed to maintain their lifestyle, plus any needed principal in case of any kind of emergency.

At the surviving spouse's death, the remaining trust assets will pass to your children in protected trusts.

You can determine how much control your child will have over the principal and income in his or her trust. The trustee, or caretaker of the trust, can buy and sell any investments within the trust, and distribute as much money to your child as needed.

If you were going to leave your money to your heirs directly, you can make your child the trustee of his own trust so he can control the trust assets without difficulty. We also add into the trust the ability for your son to name another trustee instead of himself if needed for an additional layer of creditor protection.

Perhaps if your child is a spendthrift or has drug or alcohol problems, you don't want them to control their own trust funds. Or, they have a spouse who might exert undue influence on your child to break the trust and remove all of the money from the trust so that spouse can then control and have access to the funds. In these instances, another way a trust can help protect your family is to name someone else to be the trustee, or caretaker of that money for that child's behalf.

You have many options available to you when choosing a trustee to take care of your children. You can choose one of your other children or another relative that you have confidence in... A few words of caution here — sometimes naming a sibling or another relative as trustee may lead to fighting amongst family members after you're gone. Also, you may not want to choose a person who is too much older than your child. You want that person to be around to take care of your child for a long time.

Another option is to choose a professional trustee to take care of your family's trusts and there are many options available to you regarding professional trustees.

One professional trustee option that some people choose is a bank. However, banks tend to be expensive, and sometimes stingy when doling out trust money to your child. Also, banks often invest the trust funds in CDs and other bank products, which may not be the best investment options available at the time.

Craig Kirsner's concerns about a professional trustee:

I met with someone who had a trust set up by an attorney with assets he inherited from his dad's estate. His dad named a large bank as the trustee, or caretaker of that trust, to give money to his son while he was alive.

The bank put the majority of his money in that particular bank's CDs and the stock-market based investments were all mutual funds from that particular bank's investment company's mutual funds.

The potential concern with using banks as professional trustees is that on top of the potentially high fees you might have to pay them for their services, that they could also use a lot of their own products which may or may not be the right fit for your family.

Another professional trustee option you can choose is a trust department of a brokerage firm. Again, this could be expensive and often the people working in the trust department change a lot so there often isn't a real relationship created with your child. One of my clients called this the "revolving door" of trustees.

Another good option may be for you to choose an attorney or a CPA to be your trustee.

Attorneys and CPAs are bound by the "fiduciary" rules as a professional trustee to act in your children's best interests. And often their hourly fees might be less than what a bank or brokerage firm might charge as a flat fee to manage the trust you leave your child.

If you do choose a CPA or attorney as a professional trustee, in your trust you can also suggest whom you want to be the financial advisor for the trust. That way, the financial advisor you work with now can also work with the CPA or attorney trustee to properly administer your trust in accordance with your wishes after you're gone.

CHAPTER SIX

Protect Your Grandchildren

I t's very important to my clients that their assets stay in their family bloodline. They typically don't want money to go to a child's spouse; they want their money to go to their grandchildren. On any given day you can take or leave your children, but you always love your grandchildren! Stuart Kirsner often jokes that he should have had his grandchildren first!

As mentioned earlier, many trusts are what I consider to be essentially outright distribution plans, which means your grandchild could inherit money as early as age eighteen or twenty-one, and unfortunately what they do with the money might make you roll over in your grave! Our trusts are designed so that if your children or grandchildren are under the age of thirty and are going to inherit money, then the money is held in trust for their benefit, but that child doesn't control their trust funds until at least age thirty or thirty-five ... you choose the age. My clients like that dynasty trust protection which safeguards young adults.

I'm sure you want your grandchild to be a functioning member of society. I believe that one of the surest ways to not have that happen is to give an eighteen-year-old lots of money. They might drop out of college, or get into partying and drug use. I've seen it happen many times, which is why it's so important to protect your loved ones.

Craig Kirsner discusses the potential benefits of Jack's trust:

One of my clients died and left $500,000 to each of his two grandchildren. He had a dynasty estate plan that Jack Owen set up. For his granddaughter who became our client, Jack put the $500,000 in the protected dynasty trust for the granddaughter.

This way the $500,000 in Jack's trust is designed to help protect her from lawsuits, creditor claims and divorce.

One potential big advantage to this is that she just got married and she didn't have to worry about doing a pre-nup because that $500,000 of assets are already protected from divorce!

And those trust assets are also bloodline-protected as well!

On the other hand, my client's grandson didn't put his $500,000 in a trust-based account, he chose to move the assets into his own name, which he has the right to do as trustee of his trust. However, these assets are no longer asset-protected or bloodline-protected. Hopefully this won't be an issue for him in the future. However, as my grandma always said, "hope for the best but plan for the worst!"

This example is provided for illustrative purposes only and should not be construed as advice designed to meet the particular needs of an individual's situation.

Depending on the client's assets and other factors, a good quality trust and the other important documents discussed below cost a lot less money in attorney's fees than probate costs!

A good set of complete legal documents may cost anywhere between $2,500 for a single person to $4,000 for a couple or more in attorney's fees. You can get them done for less; however, you typically don't get the dynasty provisions that my clients want.

With these documents in place and proper retitling of assets, my clients may avoid both the expense and publicity of probate, provide a more immediate transfer of wealth, and establish substantially greater control and protection of their legacy.

CHAPTER SEVEN

State Estate and Income Taxes

With the estate-tax-free exemption so high today, the reality is that a very small percentage of Americans will pay estate taxes at this time.

However, there are several states that charge you state estate taxes, which might be something that could affect your family.

The U.S. states that have state inheritance taxes include:[9]

1. New York
2. New Jersey
3. Connecticut
4. Massachusetts
5. Minnesota
6. Pennsylvania
7. Washington, D.C.
8. Illinois

---

[9] Sandra Block, Rocky Mengle and Bob Niedt. *Kiplinger.* October 27, 2022. "18 States with Scary Death Taxes."
https://www.kiplinger.com/retirement/inheritance/601551/states-with-scary-death-taxes

9. **Vermont**
10. **Maine**
11. **Nebraska**
12. **Rhode Island**
13. **Maryland**
14. **Oregon**
15. **Hawaii**
16. **Iowa**
17. **Kentucky**
18. **Washington**

A Dynasty Trust Could Save Your Heirs State Income Taxes!

One other potential advantage to a dynasty trust is that it could be set up to save your family state income taxes in the future.[10]

If you inherit a trust from someone living in a different state, the taxes you pay could either be based on your state's rate or theirs. The specifics vary a great deal by state law.[11] The taxation of the trust may depend on where the trust was created, your location or domicile when you created the trust, your trustee's location and/or the location of the beneficiary(s). Every state is different. So be sure to work with an attorney with experience and a focus on estate and tax planning and the use of trusts.

---

[10] Mark P. Cussen. *Investopedia*. September 30, 2021. "How Wealth Accumulators Can Use Trusts to Avoid State Income Tax." https://www.investopedia.com/articles/retirement/07/reduce-estate-tax.asp

[11] Richard Yam, J.D.. March 16, 2021. "How Are Trusts Taxed? FAQs." https://www.wealthspire.com/blog/how-are-trusts-taxed/

CHAPTER EIGHT

The Importance of Beneficiary Designations

C ontinuing with the topic of trusts, something to remember is to keep it funded after it's been set up. In my thirty-three years in this business, I've had numerous clients come to me assuming they have protected their assets with a trust. But quickly after looking through their paperwork, nothing has been updated. The client might not have retitled the assets or updated the paperwork. Never forget that you're the one who determines the value of those assets. If you don't take responsibility for your trust, it's just valueless paper.

It's also important to remember that beneficiary designations overrule what is stated in your will or trust. Take a life insurance policy, for example. What if, when you bought it fifteen years ago, you wrote your ex-wife's name on the beneficiary line? You guessed it, that policy will pay out in her favor.

Or, how about the thousands of dollars in your IRA you dedicated to "children" 30 years ago, but one of your children was killed in a car accident, leaving his wife and two toddlers behind? That IRA is probably going to transfer its assets to your remaining children, with nothing for your daughter-in-law and grandchildren. That's because many IRAs pay beneficiaries on a "per capita" basis, not a "per stirpes" basis. Per stirpes means that if your child predeceases you, that child's children would receive his or her portion of the inheritance. That is what most people want, but unfortunately, if done wrong, you could disinherit your grandchildren.

Because your beneficiary designations overrule your will or trust provisions, this means that even if you set up a dynasty trust but your assets' beneficiary designations name your children as beneficiaries instead of your trust, you end up having an outright distribution plan for those with assets that are not protected in your dynasty trust.

We often see this problem in second marriage situations, where the husband wants to leave some of his assets to his new wife. However, if he failed to update his beneficiary designations, when he dies, his assets would have to go to his named designated beneficiaries, potentially leaving the new wife with fewer assets than anticipated.

Craig Kirsner discusses why it's so important to make sure your beneficiary designations are up to date:

My dad and I met with a very nice couple several years ago who lived on the West Coast of Florida in Naples.

This was a second marriage and the husband's wish at his death was to leave $400,000 of his assets to his second wife and $600,000 to his three children when he died. These beneficiary wishes were exactly what his revocable living trust stated that he wanted to have happen.

Unfortunately, he died unexpectedly about six months later, without hiring us as his financial planning team.

When we met with his wife a few months after his death, she shared with us that unfortunately his beneficiary designations on his accounts did not reflect the wishes he had above. His beneficiary designations still named his three children as the beneficiaries on most of his accounts, so when he died, his wife only inherited about $100,000 in a joint account that they owned together.

This was not nearly enough money for the financial security that he wanted to leave his second wife.

This example is provided for illustrative purposes only and should not be construed as advice designed to meet the particular needs of an individual's situation.

Remember that beneficiary designations overrule trust provisions so it's very important that your entire plan is done right!

CHAPTER NINE

How to Fund
Your Living Trust

Non-IRA assets, which are considered non-qualified assets, include bank accounts, brokerage accounts, real estate, etc. They can be retitled tax-neutrally into the name of your trust. After your trust is set up, you simply take your trust to the bank or brokerage house and tell them you want to retitle the asset into the name of your revocable trust.

You can also change the beneficiary on any beneficiary-designated assets to make your spouse the primary beneficiary (if applicable), and your revocable trust the contingent beneficiary. That way when you die, your assets designated to go to contingent beneficiaries will flow into your trust so that your beneficiaries receive the creditor protection and bloodline benefits of the trust. This beneficiary update is also applicable to assets such as life insurance policies and non-qualified annuities. Remember, it's very important you update the designated beneficiaries to "fund" your trust.

Assets such as real estate can be moved into your trust with a Warranty Deed so the real estate avoids probate. In Florida, where I live, this doesn't affect your homestead rights or tax breaks, but you should check in your state with a local professional to make sure that is the case.

Also, if you have a mortgage, sometimes the bank has certain requirements and may charge a fee to retitle the mortgage into the trust. So make sure you check with your bank first before you retitle bank-financed real estate into your trust.

Assets such as IRAs and other qualified plans need to pass by beneficiary designation as described in the following chapter.

CHAPTER TEN

You Can Leave Your IRA to Your Trust

Your IRA should be asset-protected from creditor claims while you're alive... IRAs are creditor-protected in Florida! However, recent court rulings have declared inherited IRAs (an IRA that you inherit from a parent or grandparent) are NOT asset protected!

So, to protect your IRA for your heirs, you'll want to instead leave your IRA to your spouse as the primary beneficiary, if applicable, and then make the contingent beneficiary the dynasty trust set up for your children's behalf (see below for suggested wording instructions on this). However, it's very important that your trust has the latest IRA language in it so it can receive the IRA and maintain it as an IRA within the trust.

Some people might be under the belief that you're not able to leave an IRA to a trust. However, this is no longer the case as long as the trust has the latest IRA see-through "conduit" or "accumulation" language in it.

If you don't have the latest IRA provisions in your trust and you leave your IRA to your trust, it is possible the children might have to cash in the IRA and pay lump sum taxes at your death.

Important note: As of 2020 you can no longer do a stretch IRA for most non-spouse beneficiaries (with a few exceptions), so see Section 3 of this book to read Craig's article titled the "7 IRA and tax planning strategies to consider now," as seen on Kiplinger, Fidelity, Yahoo! Finance and Nasdaq.[12] The most important thing to keep in mind is that for tax purposes it's much better to leave Roth IRAs to your trust than regular IRAs. I believe you should generally leave both your regular IRAs and Roth IRAs to your trust however for tax purposes it's much better to use Roth IRAs. See Section 3 of this book for more information on this topic.

How to Leave Your IRA to Your Trust

Recent case law leads us to recommend updating the beneficiary designations on your IRAs or other qualified plans. Typically, to receive the advantages of the trust, you make your spouse the primary beneficiary of the IRA and your revocable trust the contingent beneficiary.

However, we generally recommend you update your IRA contingent beneficiary designation to be more specific so that it names each of your children's separate shares of your revocable trust that will be funded upon the second to die between you and your spouse with the percentage for each child.

An example for Joe Smith, his spouse Jane Smith, and their two children, Jim and Mary, follows:

- Primary beneficiary for Joe's IRA: Jane Smith, surviving spouse, 100%

---

[12] Media outlets do not recommend or endorse the author or the content of this book. Media appearances were obtained through a PR program. The outlets were not compensated in any way.

- Secondary or contingent beneficiaries for Joe's IRA are the separate share trusts created for the benefit of his children from Joe's and Jane's joint revocable trust as follows: The Smith Family Revocable Trust for the benefit of (FBO) Jim Smith, 50%; and The Smith Family Revocable Trust FBO Mary Smith, 50%.

Every financial institution has different requirements on how the beneficiary designations will be accepted for IRAs and other retirement plans in which they are the administrator, so it is very important to coordinate with the financial institution administrator on how they will allow beneficiary designations.

In certain circumstances with certain IRA custodians, you may have to only name the trust as the secondary beneficary without designating the separate share trusts created for the children. It depends on the IRA custodian and either way will work.

If the trust has the correct language, the trustee then can allocate your IRA and/or other retirement plan assets to your children in accordance with your wishes.

Remember, these retirement assets will be subject to income taxes to be paid by the beneficiaries once the money is received because the client put these assets away in a tax-deferred manner and income taxes were never paid on these assets.

CHAPTER ELEVEN

Revocable Versus Irrevocable Trusts

R emember that choosing to have a trust is optional. But for many, it can be an incredibly valuable asset in a portfolio.

If you do choose to have a trust, there will be several decisions you have to make about how you want it set up. First, you'll be able to decide whether you want the trust to be revocable (with changeable rules) or irrevocable (with unchangeable rules).

A brief note here about irrevocable trusts: Some people have been transferring their assets to an irrevocable trust with the help of an elder law attorney so that, technically, they don't have any assets and might qualify for Medicaid assistance for long-term care needs.

These irrevocable trusts are still subject to Medicaid look-back periods. This means if you transfer your assets into an irrevocable trust to shelter them from a Medicaid spend-down, these assets may still be considered your assets for eligibility purposes for Medicaid coverage for up to five years after the assets were transferred to the irrevocable trust.

Yet, a properly created and funded irrevocable trust can avoid both probate and estate taxes, and it can even protect assets from legal judgments against you.

The major downside of this irrevocable type of planning is that you're giving up control of your assets when they are transferred to an irrevocable trust to someone else, and most of my clients don't want to give up control of their assets while they're alive.

Assets transferred to an irrevocable trust are considered gifts to the beneficiaries of the trust at the time of the transfer and could be subject to federal gift taxes or the use of a person's federal lifetime exemption for estate taxes. Therefore, the assets transferred to an irrevocable trust are removed from the estate of the transferor, which can be beneficial for possibly lowering estate taxes. As of 2023, the federal lifetime exemption for each person is approximately $12.9 million, or $25.8 million per couple.[13]

Keep in mind that the current tax cuts are set to expire at the end of 2025 so the estate tax exemption is currently set to go back to closer to $6 million per person under current law.[14]

If you do have a substantial estate over $12.9 million or $25.8 million per couple, or over $6 million past 2026, there are some special planning techniques we can assist you with to help minimize future estate taxes.

---

[13] IRS.gov. January 2023. "What's New-Estate and Gift Tax." https://www.irs.gov/businesses/small-businesses-self-employed/whats-new-estate-and-gift-tax

[14] Investopedia. December 27 2022 "How the TCJA Tax Law Affects Your Personal Finances" https://www.investopedia.com/taxes/how-gop-tax-bill-affects-you/

CHAPTER TWELVE

What's the Downside to a Dynasty Revocable Trust?

W hen you die and the asset-protected and bloodline-protected trusts are established for your children and/or grandchildren, one downside is that the trust has to file a federal income tax return each year if it earns any income. In my opinion, that's a small price to pay for all the protection you get. However, if the trust assets go under a certain threshold, for example $100,000, the trustee has the right to terminate the trust and distribute the assets to the beneficiaries to avoid having to file a tax return on this "small" trust.

Another downside is that trusts pay more income taxes on income earned than a person would. To help address this, the trust can simply distribute all the income it earns each year to your beneficiary, and then the trust would pay no taxes and your beneficiary would pay the taxes at their normal income tax bracket.

CHAPTER THIRTEEN
Wills

Perhaps the most basic document of legacy planning, a will is a legal document wherein you state how you want your estate to be distributed. Without a will or trust, your loved ones are left behind guessing what you would have wanted, and the court will split your assets according to whatever the state's defaults are. A will or trust is important so you can avoid unintended consequences such as: even if you told your nephew that he could have your car he's been driving, if it's not in writing it still might go to the brother, sister, son, or daughter with whom you might not be communicating.

However, a will alone can be a ticket to the probate court, so your assets will be subject to probate. In probate, a judge or other potential beneficiaries can go through your will to question if it conflicts with state law, if it is the most up-to-date document, if you were mentally competent at the time the will was signed, etc. Probate may take years to settle, all the while subjecting your assets to court costs and attorney's fees.

One other undesirable piece of the probate process is that it can be a public process. That means someone can go to the courthouse, ask for copies of the case, and find out a lot about your assets, as well as who the beneficiaries are and who is disputing the will, etc.

Famous author Tom Clancy died a few years ago with only a will and no trust. And due to one sentence that wasn't clear in his will, the case went all the way to the highest court in Maryland for a decision. This one unclear line cost his children an additional $8 million in estate taxes they had to pay. And his will became public record, so anyone can see who inherited what assets.[15] [16]

Most of my clients want their wishes and their assets private, which is why they use a revocable living trust instead of a will to avoid probate.

Even with a revocable trust, you still need to have what's known as a "pour-over" will, which simply states that if you forgot to put something into your trust while you're alive, then when you die the assets are "poured" into the trust at death. However, the assets not in the trust that are poured into the trust at death may need to go through the probate process first.

The probate process often causes long unnecessary delays and commonly adds tremendous professional fees to the administration of your estate at death. Having your assets owned in your living trust during your lifetime minimizes all these costs and delays.

The next page shows an example of what happens when you have to probate a will.

---

[15] Andy and Danielle Mayoras. The Probate Lawyer Blog. Aug. 30, 2016. "Tom Clancy Estate Battle Ends, But Valuable Lesson Remains." http://www.probatelawyerblog.com/2016/08/tom-clancy-estate-battle-ends-but-valuable-lesson-remains.html

[16] Lorraine Mirabella. The Probate Lawyer Blog. Aug. 10, 2020. "Tom Clancy's Chesapeake Bay estate in Calvert County sells for $4.9 million." https://www.baltimoresun.com/business/bs-bz-tom-clancy-chesapeake-bay-estate-sale-20200811-ptto6s5zxjdovhe3vsweorojbe-story.html

Craig Kirsner's probate concerns:

One of my clients is a widowed female who was surprised to find out her husband left her $1,500,000 of investment assets when he recently died! She had no idea they had done so well accumulating wealth during their lifetime because her husband never told her.

In fact, when they went on a cruise, her husband made her pay for half the cruise out of her own money! So you can imagine that she was shocked and surprised at the amount she was inheriting from her late husband.

We contacted all eight accounts her husband left her, but unfortunately one of the accounts worth approximately $125,000 didn't name her as the beneficiary on that account... there was no "payable on death" beneficiary named.

So our client had to hire a specialist probate attorney just to do a probate for this one account. Probate means "to prove," and they had to go through the judicial process to prove that her husband wanted his wife to inherit this one account! The wife had to spend $6,500 in legal fees and court costs and it took her four months and a trip to the courthouse just so she could inherit that one account.

This is totally avoidable with proper beneficiary planning. Make sure your beneficiary designations are accurate!

This example is provided for illustrative purposes only and should not be construed as advice designed to meet the particular needs of an individual's situation.

This is why you want to fund your living trust completely while you're alive so that the least amount of assets passes through your will (ideally none).

CHAPTER FOURTEEN

Specific Gifts to Loved Ones

When you have a trust or will, in Florida you can create a separate "List of Specific Devises" signed and dated by you. This is simply a list of specific personal property assets that you want to go to specific people. These gifts can include jewelry, artwork, collections, cars, or any other personal property items you want to go to a specific beneficiary.

A Craig Kirsner Family Story:

About 90 years ago, my great-great grandfather died in Arizona and he didn't leave a list of who should get his personal belongings such as his jewelry. There was a particular ring that his mother left him and many family members on both sides of the family really wanted that particular ring. Unfortunately he didn't leave specific instructions on who should get that ring and so both sides of his family fought and broke up over this $200 valued wedding ring because it had sentimental and emotional value! Don't leave a mess for your family after you're gone.

It is very important to make this list of who should get your personal items to make things simpler at these tough times.

Taking the time to make this handwritten list could lead to a lot less stress for your family after you're gone.

You can take pictures of the items and put them on a page, or descriptions of the item including who gets what item, then sign it and date it and keep it with your will or trust. This is a legally binding part of your estate plan. The great news is that you don't need to see a lawyer whenever you change this list. Simply keep the latest list with your estate planning documents so that the list can be located by your estate administrators upon your death.

CHAPTER FIFTEEN

Other Vital Estate Planning Documents: Powers of Attorney

A power of attorney, or POA, is a document allowing another person to make medical or financial decisions on your behalf and in your best interest. They come in handy in situations where you cannot be present (think, vacation where you get stuck in Europe) or if you develop dementia or another illness that takes away your ability to make decisions for yourself.

I cannot emphasize enough how important it is to designate your powers of attorney. You never know what might happen. You might know someone or have seen a person on TV who went through immense trauma and ended up incapacitated. Your cable, Wi-Fi, and mortgage companies will still want your money, whether you are able to pay the bills or not. Having a POA in place helps everything to run as smoothly as possible when you are unable to. The person designated in your power of attorney, or POA, would have the authority to make sure your mortgage gets paid or cancel your cable while you are unable to. If properly structured, a POA can allow the person designated to carry out your estate planning wishes.

A Jack Owen Client Story:
I once spoke to a client about creating a dynasty trust for her son and grandchildren. Before she could sign the trust, she had a stroke and was unable to act on her own behalf. Because of the properly structured POA, her son as the person designated in the POA was able to sign the dynasty trust on his mother's behalf.

Multiple POAs

Let's say someone named John had three sons. He put great value on his childrens' ideas and opinions; he trusted them with his life. John didn't want to have to choose between the three children to designate as a POA, so instead he jointly appointed each of them. Now whenever those children need to make a decision for John, anything in writing needs all three signatures. We generally don't recommend having more than one POA to handle your financial decisions if you weren't able to do so yourself. This is because all of the people you chose may have to sign checks together, make joint phone calls to brokers to buy or sell investments, etc., which generally makes things more complicated to handle your finances. And what if one person is on vacation or can't be reached? It really adds a lot of complexity to choose more than one person to make your financial decisions for you.

Very importantly, we never recommend having two, let alone three POAs for emergency health care decisions, because if there was a health emergency, whichever backup you've named that the doctor can reach first has to make a quick decision — operate or don't operate. You want to have multiple backups but give each the ability to act independently as discussed in the next paragraph.

Independently Acting POAs

Let's say John had a second chance to designate his POAs. What should he do differently? Instead of needing every son to make decisions, he can authorize his sons independently. Whichever son is the most readily available at that time is the one who gets to make the decision.

POAs with different responsibilities.

What this looks like: Although Luke's daughter Claire, a nurse, was his go-to and POA for health-related issues, financial matters usually made her nervous, so he appointed his son, Matt, as his POA in all his financial and legal matters.

In addition to POAs for financial matters, another very important document to have is an advanced medical directive designating a health care surrogate. This is simply a document that points out what choices you've made about certain common health problems. Having an advanced medical directive is another one of those parts of estate planning that will help your family immensely in the time of a crisis.

Further, a designation of health care surrogate designates a person to speak with your doctors and make health care decisions on your behalf when you are unable to communicate with your doctors.

Also very importantly, we never recommend having two, let alone three health care surrogate designations for emergency health care decisions, because if there was a health emergency, the doctor may have to speak to all designated persons before he or she can act. It is probably better to have one health care surrogate designation so that whichever backup you've named that the doctor can reach first has to make a quick decision — operate or don't operate. You want to have multiple backups but give each the ability to act independently.

Living Will — Your "Pull the Plug" Wishes

Another health-related document is a living will, which is your "pull the plug" wishes. Many people agree that if two doctors certify that you're brain-dead, with no chance of recovery, that it's okay for a family member to take the relative off life support.

One recent famous example of someone not having the proper estate planning documents was Terri Schiavo. She didn't have a written living will. She was in a coma for fifteen years but because she didn't have a written living will, she could not be pulled off life support for many years of while her case when through the court system.[17]

It's really important to have your wishes in writing so your family doesn't have to deal with potentially expensive and time-consuming judicial proceedings.

---

[17] Wikiepedia, accessed March 2, 2023. "Terri Schiavo Case." https://en.wikipedia.org/wiki/Terri_Schiavo_case

CHAPTER SIXTEEN

Memorial Instructions — What Should Your Family Do With Your Body Upon Death?

D uring a period of your disability or in the event of your death, your loved ones are often not able to think very clearly. Some of these big decisions must be made within hours of death. So any help you can provide them will be very much appreciated to keep their lives simplified. Putting your wishes in writing in advance allows you to provide important information to your family and loved ones regarding your memorial instructions.

You may want to include your burial or cremation wishes and a description of the kind of memorial service you would like. You may also desire to express your feelings about the general amounts that should be spent for these remembrances. Or you may have made pre-arrangements that should be described.

You may want to leave a personal memorial letter to your family that includes the following information:

Religious affiliations, pre-purchased plans, desire for private service or service for friends and relatives, pall bearers, viewing wishes (open or closed), scripture readings, music selections, etc.

This document should say whether you want to be buried or cremated and the location and contact information for the service that you have chosen, if applicable.

Again you want to make this challenging, emotional time as easy as possible for your family, many of whom never had to deal with anything like this before (hopefully!)

CHAPTER SEVENTEEN

A Survivor's Checklist: Things That Should Be Done When a Loved One Dies

IMMEDIATELY:

- ✓ Obtain signed death certificate and autopsy records (if applicable).
- ✓ Within the first twenty-four hours, look for organ donation records. Check for signed authorization (on the driver's license or health care surrogate) and arrange immediately.
- ✓ Inventory safe deposit boxes and personal papers of the deceased. Look for burial insurance policies, prepaid mortuary or cremation society plans.
- ✓ Contact mortuary to make burial (or cremation) and funeral arrangements. Arrange for obituary notice.
- ✓ Contact friends and relatives — ALLOW YOUR FRIENDS AND RELATIVES TO HELP YOU OUT IN THIS TIME OF NEED.
- ✓ Make arrangements for pets (if any).
- ✓ Cancel regular elder assistance services, if any (such as Meals on Wheels).
- ✓ Obtain certified copies of the death certificate from the mortuary (consider purchasing ten to twenty copies).

WITHIN 30 DAYS:

- If applicable, notify:
  - ✓ Social Security Administration to stop checks (800-772-1213, www.socialsecurity.gov)
  - ✓ Medicare, generally Social Security will notify of the death. However, if the deceased was receiving Medicare Part D, had a Medigap or a Medicare Advantage plan you should contact the number on the back of their card.
  - ✓ Veterans Affairs (800-827-1000, www.VA.gov)
  - ✓ Payers of any pensions (such as a former employer), or annuities
  - ✓ Department of Motor Vehicles to cancel driver's license to minimize identity theft
  - ✓ Notify credit reporting agencies to minimize identity theft — Equifax 866-349-5191, Experian 888-397-3742, and Transunion 855-681-3196
  - ✓ Postal service to forward mail
- Locate documents, including: will, trust(s), insurance policies and deeds to real estate
- If there was a Revocable Trust, contact:
  - ✓ Successor trustee (trust manager) for eventual distribution of assets
  - ✓ **Contact Kirsner Wealth Management (1-800-807-5558)** for review of possible death and/or income taxes owing and assistance in sorting out and distributing assets along with your attorney or accountant
  - ✓ Insurance companies and arrange for any death benefits to be paid to beneficiaries
  - ✓ IRA and pension companies for any death benefits to be paid to beneficiaries
- If there was NO trust, only a Will, contact:
  - ✓ County clerk and deposit the original Will within thirty days

✓ Executor to begin the probate process with an estate planning probate attorney

✓ **Contact Kirsner Wealth Management (1-800-807-5558)** for review of possible death and/or income taxes owing and assistance in sorting out and distributing assets along with your attorney or accountant

WITHIN 60 DAYS:

✓ Notify all creditors and utility companies
✓ Transfer title on jointly held assets
✓ Inventory personal effects and arrange for disposition to family members, friends or charities
✓ Check the three credit reporting agencies to make sure no fraudulent accounts have been opened
✓ Cancel email and social media accounts
✓ Cancel memberships in organizations
✓ Notify your election board

WITHIN SIX MONTHS:

• **IF SURVIVING SPOUSE:**
✓ **Contact Kirsner Wealth Management (1-800-807-5558)** for review of finances and revised financial plan (e.g., replace lost pension, review remaining assets, etc.)
✓ Update your Will or Trust and other core legal documents (health care surrogate, durable powers of attorney, and living will) with your attorney.

From the Kirsner Wealth Management Team

CHAPTER EIGHTEEN

Estate Taxes and Income Taxes

W hen it comes to building a legacy that can last for generations, taxes can be one of the biggest drains on the impact of your hard work.

For 2023, the federal estate exemption is $12.9 million per individual and $25.8 million for a married couple, with estates facing up to a 40% estate tax rate after that.[18] According to Forbes, these limits will continue to inflate until the beginning of 2026. At that point, the limits will decrease back to the limits in 2017, which is less than half of the current limits.[19]

If you have a substantial estate, there are some special planning we can help you with now to proactively help minimize future estate taxes.

---

[18] IRS.gov. January 2023. "What's New-Estate and Gift Tax." https://www.irs.gov/businesses/small-businesses-self-employed/whats-new-estate-and-gift-tax

[19] Forbes. October 18, 2022. "Lifetime Estate And Gift Tax Exemption Will Hit $12.92 Million In 2023." https://www.forbes.com/sites/janetnovack/2022/10/18/new-higher-estate-and-gift-tax-limits-for-2023-couples-can-pass-on-extra-172-million-tax-free/?sh=26efa56b7dd8

Aside from these limits, there are also many other fees, taxes, and regulations set around the distribution of assets.

For example, consider your retirement accounts like your 401(k). There are so many things that might happen if you or an heir tamper with those funds incorrectly. Any time you try to take a large amount out of an IRA fund the IRS will probably demand a tax. Something else that might happen is an RMD, or required minimum distribution, which can and will happen whether you are still alive or not. If you pass away, you can pass on the account to a spouse and that spouse can then keep the RMDs coming. Something else your spouse can do is retitle the account, and then receive those RMDs in their own time, rather than yours.

Remember, if you don't take your RMDs, the IRS will take up to 25% of your required distribution. They have also created a new rule that if you take your missed RMD timely, the penalty is only 10%.[20]

In addition, you will still have to pay income taxes whenever you withdraw that money. However, if you are single, divorced or widowed, or your surviving spouse will simply not need the money, you could also make a younger family member the beneficiary of your retirement account through the dynasty trust we mentioned above. It used to mean the government will recalculate RMDs based on that younger person's lifespan however, due to the new Secure Act, this has completely changed.[21]

---

[20] CNBC. Greg Iacurci. Jan 3, 2023. "Secure 2.0 changes 3 key rules around required withdrawals from retirement accounts." https://www.cnbc.com/2023/01/03/3-changes-in-secure-2pointo-for-required-minimum-distributions.html

[21] Fidelity. April 1, 2021. "The SECURE Act and you." https://www.fidelity.com/learning-center/personal-finance/retirement/understanding-the-secure-act-and-retirement

We can't stress how important it is that your trust has the latest IRA conduit or accumulation language in it ... one that gives your heirs the right to choose which technique they prefer to use.

Our clients have worked hard all their lives and they want to help protect their assets they've worked so hard to accumulate. They want to help protect their children from potential future divorces, lawsuits, and creditor claims. They want to help keep their assets in their family bloodline. This is what we have been doing for over forty years with strategic partners such as Stuart and Craig Kirsner and Sean Burke of Kirsner Wealth Management.

Section 2:

Help Preserve Your Assets — Retirement Planning Strategies for Millionaires

CHAPTER NINETEEN

Preservation of Principal is so Important in Retirement!

Warren Buffett's Rules of Investing

Warren Buffett, Photo by Apple Insider

Rule No. 1: Never lose money.
Rule No. 2: Never forget Rule No. 1.[22]

---

[22] Stephanie Loiacono. Investopedia. Jan. 12, 2021. "Rules That Warren Buffett Lives By." https://www.investopedia.com/financial-edge/0210/rules-that-warren-buffett-lives-by.aspx

The Past Twenty Years of the S&P 500 History

Take a look at the following chart to see how the S&P 500, a gauge of 500 company's stocks, has performed over the past 20 years:

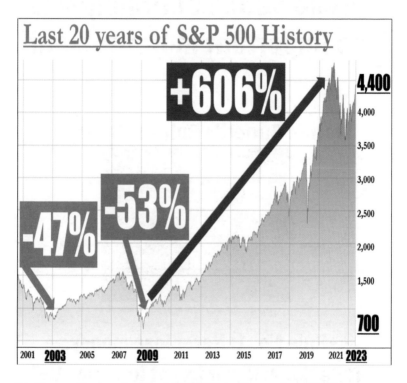

Note: It's not possible to invest directly into the S&P 500® Index; this measure is provided solely as a gauge of overall market performance. Standard & Poor's: "Standard & Poor's®," "S&P®," and "S&P 500®" are registered trademarks of Standard & Poor's Financial Services LLC ("S&P"). The historical performance of the S&P 500 is not intended as an indication of its future performance & is not guaranteed. This chart is not intended to provide investment, tax or legal advice. Be sure to consult a qualified professional about your individual situation. This chart does not take into account investment fees, so actual results may be different than depicted above. The down percentages shown above are from the top of the market to the bottom of the market in each down move without dividends. The up percentage is from March 9, 2009 through December 31, 2021 without dividends. Source: www.barchart.com/stocks/quotes/$SPX/interactive-chart.

2 Facts About the Current Market:

1. From January 1, 2009, to December 31, 2022, the S&P 500 averaged 14.1% annual returns, including dividends. Did you come to accept this as "how it should be" and become complacent?[23]

2022 was a very bad year for both stocks and bonds! With rising interest rates, higher inflation and the war in Ukraine, both stocks and bonds took a big hit. 2020 was also a very volatile year due to the Covid-19 shutdown of the global economy with an approximate 40% drop in the Dow from its highs. Since the Covid crash of March 2020, the government has pumped trillions of dollars of government bailouts into our economy which has helped propel the market back to this high. Every time the government bails us out, it might be harder for the government to bail us out again during the next recession, so personally I'm not counting on the government to bail us out every time. Are you?[24]

2. The Shiller P/E Ratio is at 30! Nobel Prize-winning professor Robert Shiller of Yale University has created this way to value the U.S. S&P 500 equity market. Historically, this ratio has been closer to sixteen. Again, right now it's at thirty. Let me put that in perspective. Over the past 148 years, we have seen PE ratios this high only THREE times: **1929, 2000, and over the past year**.[25]

---

[23] Money Chimp. "Compound Annual Growth Rate." http://www.moneychimp.com/features/market_cagr.htm

[24] TheStreet Staff. TheStreet.com. May 29, 2020. "T What Was the COVID-19 Stock Market Crash of 2020? Causes & Effects." https://www.thestreet.com/dictionary/c/covid-19-stock-market-crash-of-2020

[25] Multpl.com. Accessed on February 1, 2023. "S&P 500 Shiller PE Ratio." http://www.multpl.com/shiller-pe/

My clients have typically been riding the roller-coaster of the stock market for the past five to seven decades! At this point, they are typically retired, they're worth more than they've ever been in their life, so they want less of a roller-coaster retirement and more of a "merry-go-round" experience during retirement.

Those who are in or near retirement need to remember that stocks are designed for potential growth and non-guaranteed dividends, they are not designed for safety of your principal![26]

And never forget the brilliant words attributed to Albert Einstein: "The definition of insanity is doing the same thing over and over again and expecting a different result!"

For most of my clients, they just don't have the stomach for another 50% downturn in their retirement assets at this point in their lives so they are looking to help preserve their wealth.

---

[26] Christy Bieber. Usatoday.com. December 15, 2021. "24% of retirement savers are taking on too much investment risk. Are you one ofthem?."https://www.usatoday.com/story/money/personalfinance/retirement/2021/12/15/baby-boomers-investment-risk-retirement/49515657/?itm_source=AMP&itm_medium=UpNext

CHAPTER TWENTY

Winter is Coming: 7 Steps For A Retiree To Prepare for the Next Recession

As seen on Forbes and Kiplinger [27]

By Craig Kirsner, MBA

Just like spring and summer always lead to fall and winter, we know winter is coming and another recession is on the horizon, we just don't know when. If you have a leak in your roof when's the best time to fix that leak? <u>Before it rains</u>... because once the rain comes your house is flooded and <u>it's too late</u>.

We've seen this movie before — sky-high real estate prices coupled with sky-high stock market prices — and we have our own ideas on how it's going to end, we just don't know when. Some retirees may be concerned about going through another 2008-type of crash again at this age now that time is no longer on their side... I'm 48 years old so I have 20 more years before I even need my money, however my retired clients are living off their money today.

I believe retirees should consider being more disciplined and risk averse in the good times so you can take advantage of the bad times and not lose more than you're comfortable with when the bad times do come.

---

[27] Media appearances are paid placements. Media outlets do not recommend or endorse the author or the content of this book.

For retirees who are no longer working, their tolerance for risk at this age and stage of life has usually gone down... They've typically switched from the growth stage to the <u>distribution stage</u> where they want to help preserve their wealth and generate income from their retirement assets.

When's the right time to make sure your financial house is protected? Before the winter storm. Our brain is designed to think that if you keep doing the same thing that worked during the good times, those things will work forever... However last year was a reminder that's just not the case.

The financial advisor and investment strategy that got you to retirement might not be the right person and strategy to get you through retirement as your goals might have changed now that you're in retirement.

Since 2009, the S&P 500 has been going up almost every year for the past 14 years! Do you think the next 10 years in the economy will look like the last 10 years? We don't.[28]

<u>2022 was a rough year for both stocks & bonds</u>:

- **FAANG Stocks** **-44%**[29]
- **NASDAQ** **-33%**[30]
- **S&P 500** **-19%**[28]

---

[28] Vanguard.com. June 19, 2020. "Beyond the pandemic: What to expect from stocks, bonds." https://institutional.vanguard.com/VGApp/iip/site/institutional/researchcommentary/article/InvComBeyondPandemic

[29] PortfoliosLab.com. March 2, 2023. "FAANG Portfolio." portfolioslab.com/portfolio/faang

[30] Jesse Pound and Samantha Subin. CNBC.com. December 30, 2022. "Stocks fall to end Wall Street's worst year since 2008, S&P 500 finishes 2022 down nearly 20%." www.cnbc.com/2022/12/29/stock-market-futures-open-to-close-news.html

- **Corporate Bonds -15%**[31]

<u>2022 reminds us that markets don't go up forever.</u>

The definition of insanity is doing the same thing over and over again and expecting a different result... You want to have the right retirement plan for you, right now. Let's look at some important retirement planning and tax planning strategies for a retiree...

7 Steps For a Retiree To Help Prepare for the Coming Winter Recession:

1) How much Risk do you Want to Take in Your Retirement Plan?

It's of utmost importance to figure out how much risk you're comfortable with at this age and stage of life. We at Kirsner Wealth Management utilize industry software that can help you calculate exactly how much risk you want to take now in your retirement plan.

2) How Much Risk do you Actually Have Right Now?

It's important that as a retiree you're not taking more risk than you should. You need to analyze exactly how much risk you have in your portfolio now and that's what the industry software will show you. This software program will also show you how much you could lose with your current portfolio if you're faced with another 2008 crisis again.

---

[31] PortfoliosLab Team. PortfoliosLab.com. March 2, 2023. "iShares Core U.S. Aggregate Bond ETF (AGG)." portfolioslab.com/symbol/AGG

If you actually lost more money in 2022 than you're comfortable with, you might have more risk than you should... Most of our retired clients are no longer comfortable with too much risk at this age and stage in life.

3) How much are you paying in Fees in your Retirement Plan?

You will want to consider tuning up your retirement plan on a regular basis with the amount of risk you're comfortable with and fees that are as low as possible. Fees can considerably slow down the performance of your retirement plan and will potentially add up to a lot of money spent over time, so it's important to evaluate how much in fees, published and unseen fees you're paying. Two types of investments that might have higher fees include Mutual Funds and Variable Annuities.[32] If you own either of these, you might want to get a second opinion to be certain your fees aren't surprisingly high. Also make sure you're not paying your financial advisor too much in fees either.

4) Help Minimize Your Taxes!

As IRA professional Ed Slott says, your IRAs are "ticking tax time-bombs". Taxes might be one of the biggest expenses you have for the rest of your life, especially if you've accumulated a large IRA. This is especially true because the current tax cuts expire in 2026 so we have a limited time to take advantage of today's

---

[32] Craig Kirsner. Kiplinger.com. August 17, 2022. "7 Myths About Variable Annuities: Exposing Their Dark Side." https://www.kiplinger.com/article/retirement/t003-c032-s014-7-myths-about-variable-annuities.html

lower tax rates.[33] The fact is with your IRA it's either pay taxes now, or pay taxes later. Somebody must pay taxes on your IRA so wouldn't it be better to help pay lower taxes overall, if possible?

If you were a farmer, would you rather pay taxes on your penny seeds, or your million dollar wheat harvest? Clearly most people would rather pay taxes on the pennies, not the dollars, and that's why a Roth IRA could be a helpful strategy. This is especially important with the changes to the Stretch IRA as I discussed when I was interviewed on The Today Show recently.[34]

If you have an IRA, these are 4 reasons you might want to consider doing Partial Roth IRA Conversions each year in conjunction with your accountant:

1. Tax rates are slated to go up in 2026 so you may want to take advantage of today's low tax rates.[35]
2. If you're a married couple you're now in a joint tax bracket. When one of you passes away, the surviving spouse will be in a single tax bracket and could pay higher taxes. If the surviving spouse has a Roth IRA instead, the spouse can use that Roth IRA for living expenses without having to worry about taxes as those taxes have been paid when you were joint taxpayers.

---

[33] Amy Fontinelle. Investopedia.com. December 27, 2022 "How the TCJA Tax Law Affects Your Personal Finances." www.investopedia.com/taxes/how-gop-tax-bill-affects-you/

[34] Vicky Nguyen. Today.com. November 2, 2022 "Why Florida is losing its appeal as a prime retirement destination." https://www.today.com/video/retirement-checklist-how-to-plan-ahead-amid-rising-inflation-152271429588

[35] Amy Fontinelle. Investopedia.com. December 27, 2022 "How the TCJA Tax Law Affects Your Personal Finances." www.investopedia.com/taxes/how-gop-tax-bill-affects-you/

3. <u>For most non-spouses, the stretch IRA is gone!</u>
Your children will have to completely empty your
IRA you leave them within 10 years of your death.
An additional reason to consider converting to
Roth, as I wrote on Kiplinger,[36] your children might
have to pay higher income taxes than you as they
probably will still be working when they inherit
your IRA money.[37] Additionally, if your children
live in a state that has state income taxes, they will
have to pay those extra state income taxes as well!
The Roth IRAs can help alleviate these issues if they
arise.

4. To help preserve your assets you leave your
children, you might want to consider using a
dynasty trust as discussed in strategy #7 below. For
tax purposes you may want to consider leaving
Roth IRAs to those dynasty trusts rather than
regular IRAs. This is true whether you use a trust or
not, see strategy #7 below for reasons you might
prefer to use a dynasty trust based estate plan.

Those are four reasons you might proactively choose to
pay taxes now rather than later.

We use a software program called Holistiplan which will
help you determine the optimal amount of partial Roth
conversions you can consider doing each year. We'll work
in conjunction with your accountant to implement this
plan. And we now have a strategic partnership with a
highly experienced, licensed IRS tax preparer with over 50
years of experience that'll do our client's tax returns for
only a $175 flat fee.

---

[36] Craig Kirsner. Kiplinger.com. February 7, 2022 "Financial
Advice for Millionaires: 5 Strategies for 2022."
https://www.kiplinger.com/retirement/604177/financial-advice-for-
millionaires-5-strategies-for-2022

[37] Amy Fontinelle. Investopedia.com. December 27, 2022 "How the
TCJA Tax Law Affects Your Personal Finances."
www.investopedia.com/taxes/how-gop-tax-bill-affects-you/

5) Cut Your Expenses In Retirement

Here are some ways you can cut your expenses in retirement:

1. Downsize your home. Perhaps it's time to simplify your life?
2. Do you need a second home? With websites such as AirBNB you can rent a home anywhere in the world. Again, simplify.
3. Do you need a second car? With Uber you might not.
4. Cancel your home phone and only use a cell phone.
5. Cut your home television cable costs by looking at internet-based alternatives.

Typically, my clients are "the millionaire next door" who you'd never know have substantial wealth... They've lived below their means their entire life, which they learned from their parents who went through the Great Depression, and having done that their savings compounded over decades which have allowed them to accumulate the millions they have.

6) Make sure you're protected during retirement at the right price

Review your Long-Term Care, Umbrella Liability Insurance and Life Insurance policies to make sure you have the right protection at the right price.

In my retirement planning books, I ask that clients consider having an inexpensive Umbrella Liability Insurance policy to help protect themselves in case of a lawsuit. You can add an umbrella liability insurance policy onto your homeowner's insurance or on your auto insurance policy which will help protect you, should this happen.

If you own a life insurance policy that's more than 10 years old and qualify health-wise, you might want to review the policy to ensure it's still performing as expected.

7) Consider modernizing your estate plan with an estate planning attorney

Most of my clients have children and grandchildren whom they love dearly. We have relationships with great estate planning attorneys who can set up a dynasty revocable trust designed to help protect your assets that you leave your Children and Grandchildren from potential divorces, lawsuits and creditor claims, and help ensure your assets stay in your family bloodline. You also want to consider modernizing your Health Care Surrogate for emergency medical decisions; Durable Power of Attorney to take care of your finances in case you're disabled; and a modern Living Will which is your "pull the plug" wishes. My father, who started our business in 1972, often said when it comes to estate planning that you either buy cheap and cry forever, or buy expensive and cry once. That's true for estate planning and many things in life.

Conclusion: These 7 strategies could help set you on your path to retirement. The bottom line is to help create the greatest protection possible against loss due to economic downturns. <u>Be prepared for winter in the summer – the time to repair your roof is before the next storm.</u>

CHAPTER TWENTY-ONE

Why Use a Financial Professional?

Most of my clients have essentially "won" the game of wealth. They are retired and enjoying golf, tennis, pickleball, mahjong, bridge, canasta, spending time with their family and friends, cruises, traveling, and also going to doctor's visits. They used to think when they were still working, retirement would include all of this "free time." Yet now, they find themselves busier than ever! At this point, they are looking to simplify their lives as much as possible, so they can focus on enjoying life without worrying about things such as their retirement assets.

So, in today's world of free trades and unlimited access to information about the markets, why shouldn't people do their financial planning all by themselves? Retiring today is a lot different than retiring previously. The world used to be a simpler place, but in today's world I believe you should find a financial professional that you trust.

Your old advisor might not be the one you want during retirement

Sometimes the advisor who assisted you toward retirement is not the same one you want to guide you through retirement … your goals may have changed. Your old advisor still may have that same "growth" mentality when you're in retirement, at a time when many people's goals have changed to preservation of principal and getting income from their principal, rather than higher growth potential.

If you're a "do it yourself" investor, we often see that sometimes they employ a "follow the herd" mentality and do what everybody else is doing. That may work for a while, yet at some point the hard part is to know when it's time to change strategies by rebalancing your portfolio to ensure you're not taking on more risk than you might be comfortable with.

Perhaps your advisor put you in some kind of mutual fund or energy investment because it once paid a 12% non-guaranteed dividend. However, you might have already lost 10% or 20% or 30% of your principal!!! I think it's crazy to believe that something that might pay a 12% dividend isn't going to be as much as 6 times riskier than money in the bank earning 2%!

Or how about those Puerto Rico municipal bonds you might have lost money in? Again, the writing has been on the wall that Puerto Rico was in trouble for many years![38] Other U.S. states that might have challenges one day include New Jersey, Illinois, Kentucky, California and Connecticut, which all have less than 60% of their pensions currently funded.[39]

---

[38] Wikipedia. Accesssed March 2, 2023. "Puerto Rican government-debt crisis."
en.wikipedia.org/wiki/Puerto_Rican_government-debt_crisis

[39] Brett Arends. MarketWatch. Jan 19, 2023. "These 2 states account for a third of America's public-sector pension crisis."
https://www.marketwatch.com/story/these-2-states-account-for-a-third-of-americas-public-sector-pensions-crisis-11673964199

Many advisors and "do it yourself" investors often use a buy-and-hold portfolio.... However in today's modern, fast-paced world you want to make sure your retirement plan is solid and that it matches your current goals and needs.

We create retirement plans for our clients that are looking to make sure that their income will last for their entire lives and that they're prepared for life's unexpected issues that come up from time to time.

We do a number of things differently than the average advisor...

How much risk do you want to take now?

Since most of my clients are ages 65 to 85, my clients are much more concerned with principal preservation and income than growth at this stage in their lives. Because they're aware that the more upside they have in riskier assets, the more downside they have as well.

There are five retirement plan risk category levels that you can be in as a client of Kirsner Wealth Management...

The 5 risk levels you can take in your retirement plan are:
1) Conservative
2) Moderately Conservative
3) Moderate
4) Moderately Aggressive
5) Aggressive

Most of my clients choose to be in the <u>Moderately Conservative</u> category, with some in Moderate and a few in the Conservative category. I typically don't work with people who are looking to hit "home runs" such as the Moderately Aggressive or Aggressive categories, because the more risk you take the more upside you have, but also the more downside potential as well.

The Moderately Aggressive and Aggressive levels of risk means you have up to 100% of your money in stocks and my clients have switched from the growth stage of their lives to the distribution stage of their lives which never involves having 100% of your money at higher risk.

Our clients have gone through many up and down cycles in their lives, and they don't want to lose another big portion of their retirement money at this point in retirement.

We use technology to help our clients

We use a powerful industry software, the underlying principles of which is based on a Nobel Prize-winning framework, to help ensure our clients have the right amount of risk that they find acceptable in their retirement portfolio.[40]

In my office where we meet our clients, we have a 65-inch smartboard, which is a giant computer that we can write on and interact with while analyzing our clients' portfolios with them as shown below:

---

[40] kb.riskalyze.com. April 24, 2023. "Fiduciary Standards" https://kb.riskalyze.com/hc/en-us/articles/115009004627-Fiduciary-Standards#:~:text=Built%20on%20the%20academic%20framework ,tolerance%20and%20engineer%20portfolio%20risk

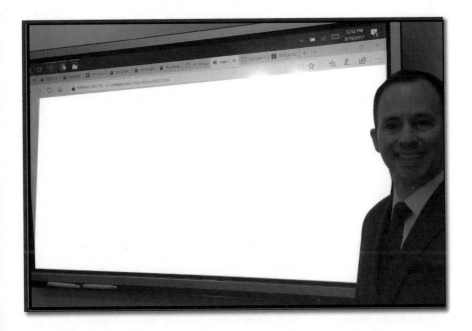

Our clients often joke that they like this giant 65 inch computer screen because they can actually read it without their glasses!

This giant computer screen is great for when we meet with clients so we can go through their retirement situation and help design a plan that fits their goals at this age and stage of their lives.

What Does the Average Investor Do?

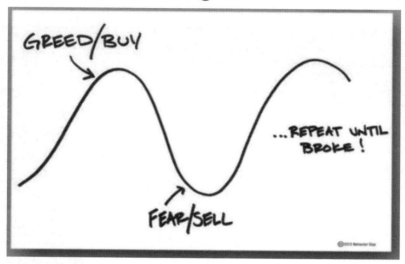

Don't be the average investor!

Unfortunately, studies have shown that the average investor buys high and sells low. This is mostly due to emotional investing.[41]

Warren Buffett, of Berkshire Hathaway, is a renowned investor who does the opposite of the above image – he likes to buy low and sell high.

Warren Buffett's company as of early 2023 has $88 billion in cash! That's much higher than the $20 billion of cash Buffett he normally has on hand.[42]

---

[41] Dana Anspach. The Balance. May 26, 2021. "Why Average Investors Earn Below Average Market Returns." https://www.thebalance.com/why-average-investors-earn-below-average-market-returns-2388519

[42] William Dahl. Yahoo Finance. March 1, 2023. "Billionaire Charlie Munger Reveals Why Berkshire Hathaway has an $88 Billion Pile of Cash." finance.yahoo.com/news/billionaire-charlie-munger-reveals-why-223714310.html

Charlie Munger, Warren Buffet's right-hand man said that Berkshire isn't buying anything "because there's nothing we can stand buying."

It's amazing that even with a stock market downturn in 2022 that would presumably result in dozens or hundreds of stocks trading on sale at bargain prices, the world's most famous value investors aren't remotely tempted to buy.

Perhaps we should take a lesson as this book is written in July 2023 and be cautious ourselves with our investments.

CHAPTER TWENTY-TWO

What Does Our 3 Bucket Retirement Financial Plan Look Like?

We create a 3 bucket retirement plan:

Our three bucket approach to setting up your retirement plan involves your following 3 buckets:

Bucket #1: Bank $. Keep between 6 months to 12 months of your yearly expenses in the bank for emergencies. For most of my clients that's between $50,000 to $100,000 in the bank.

Bucket 2: Income and Safety. This bucket is designed for income and safety of your principal. They are not all guaranteed but are generally more conservative than market-based investments.

Some typical sources of your income might include:
- Social Security
- Pension

- RMDs (Required Minimum Distributions) you've already taken
- Rental Income
- Annuity Income

Bucket 2: Income & Safety . This bucket is designed for income and safety of your principal. They are not all guaranteed but are generally more conservative than market-based investments.

Some typical sources of your income might include:
- Social Security
- Pension
- Rental Income
- Annuity Income

Our retired clients typically want to have lower risk on their retirement portfolio. Many investors have turned to bonds for lower risk investments as bonds typically have lower risk than stocks. However, bonds can go down when interest rates rise like they did in 2022, which led to a 15% drop in corporate bond values![43] So along with bonds and cash, we also might recommend fixed index annuities from large, highly rated insurance companies if appropriate.

With a fixed index annuity, you're able to earn interest that's tied to the performance of an external index such as the S&P 500 without ever being invested in the market. They also help protect from market downturns, keeping your principal safe.

Your principal has the potential to receive interest each year based on the positive growth of a separate market

---

[43] PortfoliosLab Team. PortfoliosLab.com. March 2, 2023. "iShares Core U.S. Aggregate Bond ETF (AGG)." https://portfolioslab.com/symbol/AGG

index like the S&P 500. You aren't invested in the S&P 500 directly, but the insurance company will credit your annuity interest based on the S&P 500's gains, up to limits set by the issuing company.

For example, an annuity contract based on the S&P 500's growth with a cap rate of 10% means that if the S&P 500 goes up 10% or more over the next year, you would earn 10%. If the S&P 500 goes up 7%, you get 7%. The insurance company locks in your interest earnings every year and you can never lose those locked-in interest credits.

However, because your money isn't invested in the market with a fixed index annuity, if the market nosedives (2000, 2008 and 2022), you won't see any increase in your contract value... Most importantly for a retiree, there will also be no decrease in your contract value due to that market loss (although any optional rider fees will continue to be assessed each year, if you selected to purchase them).

These guaranteed retirement strategies aren't designed to beat the stock market, they're designed to offer conservative growth potential and a vehicle to be used as part of an overall retirement plan without market risk.

Another advantage of having a guaranteed annuity as part of your retirement plan is that if bucket 3, your growth bucket is having a bad year due to a market downturn, you may be able to take money out of this guaranteed annuity to live on and give your growth bucket a chance to potentially recover. This way you may not have to sell assets in the growth bucket when they're down... you can give them a chance to recover.

Many of the guaranteed annuities we use allow you to take up to 10% of your money out each year without a surrender penalty to help you live on this money if needed to give your riskier money a chance to come back up.

If you would rather opt for safety of principal more than growth potential on a part of your retirement plan, it's possible that a fixed index annuity might work for you as part of your overall plan.

Retirees typically like the idea of a portion of their money having the opportunity to grow when their selected market index option goes up each year, but never losing that money when the markets go down. They provide principal guarantees that are backed by large, established, highly-rated insurance companies, with competitive growth potential.

We have access to over 100 insurance companies so we can work toward your needs and goals.

Bucket 3: Growth Potential. Professionally managed, diversified portfolios of Institutional Mutual Funds and ETFs. We mostly use ETFs where appropriate as they are more tax-efficient than mutual funds. ETFs also tend to have lower costs than mutual funds.

We often work with ETF fund managers such as Vanguard, Fidelity and Schwab. We also have access to Institutional Fund Managers including Pimco, Guggenheim, JP Morgan and more!

We adjust these portfolios every 4 to 6 weeks, or more often as needed.

The following image shows our 3 bucket approach to investing that's designed for a retiree to have a well diversified portfolio with retirement funds in a lot of different buckets:

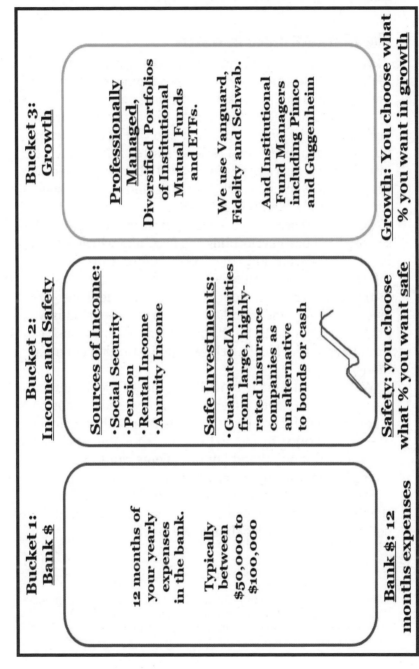

Bucket 1:
Bank $

12 months of your yearly expenses in the bank.

Typically between $50,000 to $100,000

Bank $: 12 months expenses

Bucket 2:
Income and Safety

Sources of Income:
· Social Security
· Pension
· Rental Income
· Annuity Income

Safe Investments:
· Guaranteed Annuities from large, highly-rated insurance companies as an alternative to bonds or cash

Safety: you choose what % you want safe

Bucket 3:
Growth

Professionally Managed, Diversified Portfolios of Institutional Mutual Funds and ETFs.

We use Vanguard, Fidelity and Schwab.

And Institutional Fund Managers including Pimco and Guggenheim

Growth: You choose what % you want in growth

The markets move in waves

What's interesting about the markets is that oftentimes sectors do well for a period, then those same sectors might underperform in the market for the next period.

For example, technology stocks did really well for the period from the bottom of the market in 2009 to 2021, however when the Federal Reserve started raising interest rates in 2022, tech stocks tumbled with the FAANG stocks dropping 46% in one year! (FAANG stands for Facebook, Amazon, Apple, Netflix and Google).[44]

So, our research teams send us information on which sectors have been performing the best, and which sectors have been performing the worst so we can use that information in our strategies for our clients' portfolios.

In our practice, our clients are looking for diversification[45] and liquidity. To help accomplish this we might use low-cost ETFs (exchange-traded funds) such as from Vanguard, Fidelity, Schwab and institutional mutual funds.

We're very pleased to be able to use institutional mutual funds with our clients, which are typically used by pension plans and very high net worth clients. Normally you might need $250,000 or $500,000 or more to buy an institutional mutual fund but our clients can use them in their portfolios in any dollar amount.

We like to use mutual funds and ETFs to offer our clients diversity and liquidity rather than take on the potentially higher risk of individual stocks.

---

[44] PortfoliosLab Team. PortfoliosLab.com. March 2, 2023. "FAANG Portfolio." https://portfolioslab.com/portfolio/faang

[45] Diversification does not ensure a profit or guarantee against losses in declining markets.

One of my clients told me the stock market was like his hand:

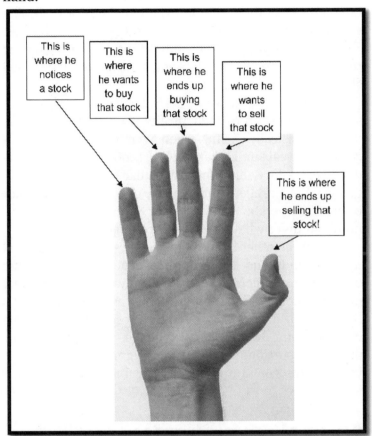

Fees

Fees can be a big drag on performance. It might not sound like much but paying too much over a twenty- or thirty-year period can greatly affect how long your retirement portfolio lasts.

As a general rule, you should avoid high-fee mutual funds. Now, many people we come across have mutual funds. There are great mutual funds out there and not-so-great mutual funds. We evaluate mutual funds based on how much risk they contain, whether the sector is doing well or not, and the expense of the mutual fund's total fees.

Why might you have a mutual fund with a higher fee than we offer our clients? It might have to do with revenue sharing.

What is revenue sharing? Many broker-dealers derive a significant portion of their profits from revenue sharing deals. It basically means when your broker sells you a certain mutual fund, that mutual fund pays the broker-dealer extra for selling that particular fund. I don't think it's fair that a broker would choose one fund over another because he gets a "kickback" for selling that particular fund, but that's what revenue-sharing means.

We, on the other hand, only use low-cost institutional mutual funds and ETFs that have no revenue sharing deals. We use Fidelity, Vanguard, Schwab or institutional mutual funds which tend to have relatively low fees.

And Sean Burke, M.S., our Vice President, watches the market daily to monitor, manage and update our diversified portfolio investments designed to help preserve your wealth in conjunction with our research-based partners.

Beware of high fees in variable annuities!

Speaking of high fees, be especially wary of variable annuities that often have high fees. Many variable annuities have fees of 2% to 3% per year.[46]

Variable annuities are not inherently bad or good, they are merely a tool that may work well for one but not

---

[46] Dana Anspach. The Balance. November 26, 2021. "5 Variable Annuity Fees to Ask About." https://www.thebalance.com/variable-annuity-fees-to-ask-about-2389027

another. However, they tend to be less appropriate for a retiree or pre-retiree due to the level of market risk and potential for market loss they include. We have a software system that analyzes mutual fund and variable annuity fees for our clients.

 To learn more about variable annuities and why we don't think they are suitable investments for many retirees, go to my website www.KirsnerWealth.com to watch a video I made about variable annuities.

How to identify a good financial advisor

When interviewing financial professionals, you want to know if they are licensed to sell securities, licensed to provide investment advice, and also licensed to offer insurance-based products, so you have access to a diversified set of strategies. You may not want to have all of one or all of the other to create a well-balanced retirement portfolio that is designed to help withstand all markets.

Also, when you go into their office, do you feel welcome? Is it nice and professional? Does it make you feel confident? Do they have nice staff? We're very pleased to declare that we have a great staff who makes sure that we really take care of our clients. We own our office-condo which is located just south of Boca Raton in Coconut Creek, Florida.

A real financial plan

It's our mission to provide all of our clients with unbiased advice that we believe is right for them. There are regulatory standards that apply to the work we do. We are an independent firm, which means we are not pressured by a large parent company to sell you on one investment over another. We focus entirely on your financial well-being and pairing you with the strategy that meets your unique needs. Our retired clients are now looking for a simpler, "slow and steady wins the race" plan. That's the stage of life they're in. They've been through the ups and downs of market cycles and never want to go through another 2008 again! We are here to help you, as we have been since my father founded our business in 1972.

CHAPTER TWENTY-THREE

Investment Strategies for the Different Stages of the Economic Cycle

As seen on Kiplinger, Fidelity, Yahoo Finance & Nasdaq.com[47]

By Sean Burke, M.S., Vice President of Kirsner Wealth Management

Our approach to investing is based on the economic cycle (See the graphic on the following page). Our economy goes through different stages of the economic cycle, where different types of investments will do better or worse. We adjust the general allocation of stocks, bonds and other investments based on where we

---

[47] Media appearances were obtained through a PR program. The outlets were not compensated in any way.. Media outlets do not recommend or endorse the author or the content of this book.

are in the cycle and where we think we are going, as well as the underlying investments in sectors. Our goal is to manage the portfolio to find the highest potential rate of return for the least amount of risk (also known as risk-adjusted returns), adding growth potential during growth periods and adding principal protection through the use of fixed insurance products in times of uncertainty.

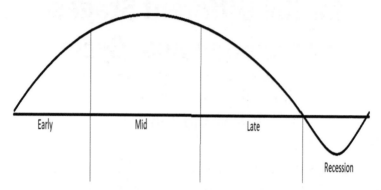

In a diversified portfolio, the allocation of stocks and bonds will generally determine the risk of the portfolio. The more stock in the portfolio the more risk. Stocks tend to do better in the early and the mid cycle, and bonds tend to do better during a recession.

The reason for that being that as investors are wary of investing in stocks, which generally carry more risk, they often look for safety in bonds. Thus, dollars shift from the stock market to the bond market, so the demand for bonds goes up therefore so can their price.

This typically provides an inverse relationship in a recession designed to add a level of protection and stability to the portfolio. There are other categories of investments that make up a much smaller piece of the portfolio but are often considered relatively stable in the late stage and recession as well, including high-yield bonds and potentially commodities. All investments involve risk and the potential loss of principal, so it's important to keep that in mind when building your retirement portfolio.

Beyond the general stock and bond allocation, we also look at what sectors do well in which parts of this cycle. In the early stage, where we are seeing high growth, usually economically sensitive sectors might outperform while more defensive sectors could underperform. Examples of economically sensitive sensors include technology, industrials, and consumer discretionary. The early part of the cycle has historically been relatively short, on average one year, and on average returned about 20% returns.[48]

The mid-cycle has been a longer stage in the economy and has averaged about three years. This stage has typically been one of steady growth where we didn't see any sector significantly outperform in this stage. This stage might be a good opportunity to reset the asset allocation to help avoid losing some of the gains made by previous growth. The average return during the mid-cycle historically has been about 14%.[40]

The late cycle is one where we might look to defensive and inflation protected categories such as materials, consumer staples, healthcare, utilities, and energy. This stage is simply a slow down from the higher growth period of the mid cycle, it does not mean that we are having negative growth in the economy, it just means we are no longer growing at the same pace. The return historically has been less, on average about 5%.[41]

In recession there are typically no sectors that do very well because stocks tend to perform poorly most of the

---

[48] Fidelity. August 12, 2022. "How to invest using the business cycle." https://www.fidelity.com/viewpoints/investing-ideas/sector-investing-business-cycle

[40] Ibid.

[41] Ibid.

time during a recession. What we look for in recession are companies that provide potential stability and are more defensive. These might include consumer staples, companies that provide goods and services that people need regardless of economic condition. A good example of this is healthcare because people need healthcare services, drugs, and care regardless of economic condition. Another example would be utilities... These are non-negotiable for people. Additionally, the more defensive companies mayhave higher dividends that help to weather the storm of recession, which has historically averaged negative 15% returns.[49]

Every market cycle is different, and we can see different sectors perform in different ways depending on the economic conditions, and we are seeing that coming out of a pandemic-inspired recession vs a typical cycle. Real estate and financials are a good example of this today, where we believe they are positioned for growth versus in 2009 where they were definitely not positioned for growth! Additionally, we can move forwards and backwards on this curve, not always in constant motion from early, to mid, to late, to recession. We use our research and indicators to determine where we are in this cycle and what sectors we believe will perform well, and we slightly tilt the allocations of the portfolios to seek the greatest risk adjusted returns.

These strategies, along with our research-based teams, are designed to allow us to help preserve our client's retirement portfolio, which is so important to our retired clients.

---

[49] Ibid.

CHAPTER TWENTY-FOUR

What Is Tactical Investing?

Remember that the markets can go up slowly like an escalator and down quickly like an elevator. That's why it's very important to be able to adjust your retirement portfolio to what's happening in the markets.

We use tactical investing to help rebalance our clients' accounts based on market conditions. Based on the one of the research models we use, the markets are in one of three conditions, Positive (Green), Neutral (yellow) or Negative (red):

So, what does this mean to you?

Let's say that you want a moderate risk portfolio. In my experience, many moderate portfolios are set up with a 70% stock exposure and a 30% bond exposure. The problem with that, in our opinion, is that when the market is doing poorly, such as in 2001-2003 and 2008- 2009, having 70% stock exposure is often too much. And then in good times in the markets such as from 2003-2008 and 2009-2018, that 30% bond portion of your plan could be a drag on your overall portfolio.

Our portfolios are different ... when the research models are saying that the markets are green or yellow, as an example, our moderate portfolios typically have a 70% exposure to stocks and 30% exposure to bonds or other asset-backed securities.

However, when the indicators flip to red, we proactively adjust our clients' portfolios and may move down accordingly.

To summarize, our moderate portfolio is generally set up in one of two ways:

- Option 1: When the market indicators are looking good, a moderately conservative portfolio might be made up of 55% equity ETFs and 45% less aggressive ETFs or mutual funds, which could include bonds, foreign bonds, asset-backed securities, muni bonds, real estate, etc. We also use Fixed, guaranteed annuities as appropriate. These assets are designed to have less risk to your principal than stocks.
- Option 2: However, in quarters where the previous quarter wasn't looking so good and the model went to red we might change our moderately conservative portfolio to a much more conservative allocation.

<u>Hypothetical</u> example shown for illustrative purposes only, is not a recommendation and your actual allocation will vary. Diversification does not ensure a profit or guarantee against losses, rather it is a method used to help manage risk.

We automatically make portfolio adjustments for our clients every 4 to 6 weeks or more often based on market conditions.

Where Did the "Bull" and "Bear" Markets Get Their Names?

The Bull, photo by Rob Kiser

A bear market refers to a market going down for a few months or few years at a time, and a bull market is when prices are rising. Where did they get their names?

When a bull attacks, it attacks from below, using its horns to throw its prey into the air.

However, when a bear attacks, it stands up tall and uses its paws to swipe down and hit its prey to the ground.

So a bull market represents an up market and a bear market represents a down market.[50]

[50] Mary Hall. Investopedia. November 30, 2021. "Where Did the Bull and Bear Market Get Their Names?"
https://www.investopedia.com/ask/answers/bull-bear-market-names/

CHAPTER TWENTY-FIVE

Can Risk Management Saves Lives?

A sudden loss of wealth can increase the risk of dying earlier, according to a study done in 2015.[51] As risk managers, first and foremost, with risk management as our mission and primary function, the purpose of our research-based models is to help identify conditions of higher risk in the markets over varying timeframes with the goal of avoiding large losses.

Let's look at the following chart, which simply illustrates the real market recovery, or gain, needed to bounce back and break even from a given percentage of market loss.

If we think back to the not-so-distant past — say, 2008 — in which many retirees and soon-to-be retirees saw market losses in excess of 30% to their accounts, you see that this meant you had to earn back a 43% gain necessary to get back to even.

---

[51] Nigel James Green. Forbes. July 3, 2020. "The Deep Connection Between Your Health and Wealth." https://www.forbes.com/sites/forbesfinancecouncil/2020/07/03/the-deep-connection-between-your-health-and-wealth/?sh=2436c4bd52aa

And if you lost 50% of your account, you'd have to earn 100% to break even!

As you can see below, the greater the percentage of loss, the more exaggerated or significant the percentage gain you would have to have just to get back to where you began:

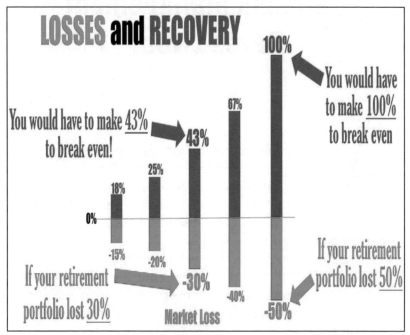

Disclaimer: The hypothetical example above is for illustrative purposes only, and should not be deemed a representation of past or future results. It isn't a guarantee of return or future performance. This example does not represent any specific product or service.

The purpose of this graphic is to illustrate that if you lost X% in the market, Y% growth is needed for you to get back to your starting value. For example, if you start with $100,000 and lose 30%, as shown in column 5, your new starting value would be $70,000. The percentage of growth needed to return to the original $100,000 is 43%, but the dollar amount of $30,000 gain is the same!

The difference is after a loss you have less capital to grow so you have to earn more to break even. This is why retirees who no longer have time on their side need to help avoid losses as much as possible.

What is the "Rule of 100" now known as the "Rule of 120"?

The "Rule of 100" is a general rule of thumb that tells you approximately how much stock exposure you should accept. If you're age seventy, you subtract your age from one-hundred. In this case, 100 - 70 = 30, so you should have no more than 30% of your portfolio in stocks. However, nowadays some people are more comfortable with the "Rule of 120", where you take your age minus 120, so a seventy-year-old could have 50% of their portfolio in stocks.

Frequently we see clients with far more risky "red assets" than that. While the strategy worked for many from 2009 through December of 2021, it generally didn't work as well in 2022, and no one knows how much longer it might continue to work before the next major downturn will occur. So if your goal is to help preserve your assets, its important that you have the right amount of risk for you.

CHAPTER TWENTY-SIX

Seven Golden Rules for Investing and Advanced Estate Planning

By Craig Kirsner, MBA

Y ou've worked hard to build your nest egg. To help preserve it, for yourselves and for your heirs, consider this set of "golden rules".

We've seen this movie before — sky-high stock prices, sky-high real estate prices and the Fed raising interest rates. We also saw how those times ended in 2001 and 2008.

At this point, my clients are looking to help preserve their wealth, so here are my five golden rules of investing and two golden rules of advanced estate planning that I share with them, which I've learned since 1994. I focus on working with retirees with over a million dollars in net worth; however, these rules can apply to everyone. Keep in mind these are for informational purposes only, they are not advice customized to your own situation and may not be appropriate for you specifically.

Five Golden Rules of Investing
Rule No. 1:

Diversification[52] can be an important part of a retirement plan, and the central measure of diversification is to not have more than 5% of your portfolio in any one position.

This is crucial because you never know if one piece of bad news, or some new technology, could come along that could potentially disrupt one company's performance and stock price.

Rule No. 2:

There are eleven sectors in the S&P 500, so I believe you should never have more than 20% of your portfolio in any one sector.

This was a big problem in the late nineties, when tech stocks did amazing and if you hadn't rediversified your portfolio before the tech bubble burst in the early 2000s, anyone with too much exposure to tech really took a beating.

We're seeing that again now because the FAANG stocks — Facebook, Amazon, Apple, Netflix, and Google (Alphabet) — have been the best performing and most widely held stocks around. Those five stocks alone make up 19% of S&P 500 market cap.[53]

If you own any highly valued stocks at this point and don't want to have as much risk, remember to keep

---

[52] Diversification does not ensure a profit or guarantee against losses during a declining market.

[53] Jason Fernando. Investopedia. June 29, 2022. "FAANG Stocks: Definition and Companies Involved."
https://www.investopedia.com/terms/f/faang-stocks.asp#:~:text=As%20of%20August%202021%2C%20the,States%20economy%20as%20a%20whole.

diversifying. Remember, I suggest investors never have more than 20% exposure to any one sector of the S&P 500.

The 11 sectors of the S&P 500 are[54]:

- Energy
- Materials
- Industrials
- Utilities
- Consumer Staples
- Health Care
- Financials
- Information Technology
- Communications
- Consumer Discretionaries
- Real Estate

Rule No. 3:

Positions that pay a dividend are generally preferable to those that don't. This means your money is working for you and paying you money along the way. On the other hand, what's important to a retiree is to make sure they're not taking too much risk, and stocks add risk to your principal. For example, keep in mind that while AT&T pays a 7% non-guaranteed dividend as of July 5, 2023, during the 2008 to 2009 financial crisis, AT&T lost 46% of its principal.[55] [56]

I've seen a number of people come to my office who bought stocks paying 10% or more in dividends, and in 2022 those stocks lost significant amounts of their principal. We often say, if a stock is paying a 10% dividend, and banks are paying 1%, you might be taking 10 times the risk to your principal over money in the bank. Think about

---

[54] Rebecca Lake. SoFi. Aug. 24, 2021. "What Are the Different S&P 500 Sectors?" https://www.sofi.com/learn/content/sp-500-sectors/

[55] Nasdaq. Jan. 31, 2023. "T Dividend History." https://www.nasdaq.com/market-activity/stocks/t/dividend-history

[56] Yahoo Finance, May 5, 2021 https://finance.yahoo.com/quote/T?p=T&.tsrc=fin-srch

it logically, if they're paying 10% dividends doesn't it make sense that might be a riskier investment?

That's why we often prefer using ETFs and institutional mutual funds with relatively low fees to help achieve diversification.

Rule No. 4:

Consider owning a reasonable portion of fixed income assets at all times, including real estate investments and fixed, guaranteed annuities. Most retirees don't want to have as much volatility in their retirement plan and this helps them achieve that goal. As I write this book in July 2023, keep in mind that we are fourteen years into this bull market in real estate, so be careful of the current risk present in the real estate market. While younger people may be fine investing in rental real estate or REITs, a retiree whose goal is to help preserve their wealth may prefer to take those high real estate prices into consideration and ramp back their position in that sector in favor of more bonds, preferred stocks or guaranteed annuities instead. As you're well aware, markets don't go up forever.

Rule No. 5:

Keep 5% of your assets in cash, because challenges happen in life. Most of my clients always have $50,000 to $75,000 of cash in the bank. It makes sense to have at least six months of expenses in your savings account.

Two Golden Rules of Legacy Planning

In addition to wanting to help preserve their wealth, my clients want to leave a legacy to their children and grandchildren after they're gone. Here are two estate planning golden rules to consider in order to create a legacy for your family in conjunction with your estate planning specialist attorney:

Estate Planning Golden Rule No. 1:

Consider a dynasty revocable trust to help protect the assets you leave to your family. The estate planning attorneys we work with set up revocable living trusts with dynasty provisions. This means that after you and your spouse are gone, a bulletproof trust is set up for each of your children that's designed to be 100% divorce, creditor, and lawsuit protected for your children. These trusts are intended to help protect the assets you leave to your children.

What's also crucial to my clients is that these trusts help keep their assets in their family bloodline. After your child passes away, the funds in the trust don't go to that child's spouse, those trust assets only go down to your grandchildren in the same bulletproof trusts. This also gives your grandchildren divorce, creditor and lawsuit protection. Very importantly, it doesn't give your grandchildren control of their money at age eighteen or twenty-one but waits until they are at least age thirty, so they don't make dumb mistakes early in life.

Estate Planning Golden Rule No. 2:

You must fund your dynasty revocable trust. After you set your trust up, you must fund it by either retitling your non-IRA assets into those trusts or changing the beneficiary of your assets so that your spouse is the primary beneficiary (if applicable) and then your trust is named as the contingent beneficiary.

If instead, you make the mistake of naming your children contingent beneficiaries, your assets will not go into those protected trusts, they will go directly into your child's name with no asset protection or bloodline protection.

What's worse, let's say you named your ex-wife as beneficiary and never changed that. When you die, your ex-wife will receive those funds even if your trust dictates otherwise. Beneficiary designations overrule trust directions.

It's imperative to find an attorney who specializes in advanced estate planning. They might be expensive, but as my dad always says with an estate plan you can buy expensive and cry once or buy cheap and cry forever. Isn't that often true with many things in life?

Keep these five golden rules of investing and two golden rules of estate planning in mind, to help you feel more confident that your retirement assets can help withstand any future challenges.

CHAPTER TWENTY-SEVEN

Financial Concerns
for a Surviving Spouse

What happens when one spouse dies:

1. The smaller Social Security payment stops.
2. A pension might stop or decrease.
3. The surviving spouse is now a single taxpayer, which means they may experience an increase in income taxes due to becoming a single filer... with only one standard deduction.

Many of our clients are married and are concerned about what will happen when one of them passes away. Statistically, women live about 6 years longer than men on average.[57]

Our clients are getting older, and unfortunately, we generally attend one or two funerals each year. After decades of service, we've gotten very good at making sure that the surviving spouse, who is typically the wife, is well taken care of and looked after. We hold their hands in these trying times and support them as part of the team updating their financial situation, their estate planning situation with the attorney, and their income tax situation with their accountant.

Typically with the majority of my married clients the husbands are more in charge of finances than the wife, on average. My concern for that wife is that if she outlives her husband, then where will she go to where they know about money? Often, she'll go to the bank.

And who might rope your wife into speaking with them but the "financial advisor" that's employed by the bank who sits in the bank waiting to help bank clients with financial advice.

My concern with that "financial advisor" and the financial planning industry in general, is that very often that financial advisor might be tempted to sell a product that might be better for him than for the client.

For example, Wells Fargo is a bank with an investment arm that comes to mind that's been in a lot of trouble lately for misleading investors... Issues were uncovered with the private bank part of Wells Fargo's wealth management business because for years Wells Fargo had operated with

---

[57] Charlotte Morabito. cnbc.com. March 1, 2023. "Here's why American men die younger than women on average and how to fix it" https://www.cnbc.com/2023/03/01/why-american-men-die-younger-than-women-on-average-and-how-to-fix-it.html

a heavy sales culture that pressured advisors to make decisions that were later determined to not be necessarily in their clients' best interest. This is also on top of millions of dollars in SEC fines for ill-gotten gains garnered from mom-and-pop investors.[58] At the end of 2022, Wells Fargo was fined another $3.7 billion dollars in fines and restitution for mismanaging consumer loans and accounts![59]

---

[58] U.S. Securities and Exchange Commission. Feb. 21, 2020. "Wells Fargo to Pay $500 Million for Misleading Investors About the Success of Its Largest Business Unit."
https://www.sec.gov/news/press-release/2020-38

[59] CPAPracticeAdvisor.com. December 21, 2022. "Wells Fargo to Pay $3.7 Billion in Fines and Restitution for Mismanaging Consumer Loans and Accounts."
https://www.cpapracticeadvisor.com/2022/12/21/wells-fargo-to-pay-3-7-billion-in-fines-and-restitution/75110/#:~:text=Home-,Wells%20Fargo%20to%20Pay%20%243.7%20Billion%20in%20Fines%20and%20Restitution,of%20those%20kinds%20of%20accounts.

Craig's potential concerns about the financial planning done by certain big banks:

I met with an eighty-two year old who wanted to simplify his life so last year he moved all of his retirement accounts to his bank's financial planning arm.

First, he was very angry to find out that the bank sold him a $200,000 variable annuity! He wasn't even aware he bought a variable annuity.

Second, he has been a bond buyer for a long time and he was very angry to find out that they sold him $150,000 of corporate bonds that he ended up paying a total of $189,000 for due to the very high 26% bond premium! He was furious as he's never paid that high of a bond premium before!

Third, he was also angry that his broker told him his annual fees on his managed money account were supposed to be 0.75% per year, however they were charging him more than twice that at 1.54% per year in management fees!

These are some of my concerns when working with a big bank's financial planners. Of course, not all banks operate this way and there are many good brokers who want to do right by their clients. But you still need to understand who you are working with, what they offer, and how much it really costs.

I am an independent financial advisor, and I am also 48, with my goal being to work in this industry another 20 to 25 years and then hopefully my sons will take over the business like I did for my dad.

It's very important that our clients are well taken care of for the rest of their lives, both the husband and wife, if applicable.

CHAPTER TWENTY-EIGHT

Have a Retirement Bucket List? Don't Hesitate to Dive In!

As seen on Kiplinger, Nasdaq and Flipboard.com[60]

By Craig Kirsner, MBA

Early in retirement is when you are most likely to have the three necessary elements going for you at the same time — money, health and time.

Retirement can be a time for relaxing and enjoying some hard-earned leisure time. It's also an opportunity to spend quality time with family and loved ones and build lasting memories with them. Retirement is also your time to finally get around to doing all those things that you've always wanted to do but have been putting off due to the pressures of

---

[60] Media appearances were obtained through a PR program. The media outlets were not compensated in any way. Media outlets do not recommend or endorse the author or the content of this book.

work or the day-to-day necessities of running a business.

For some people, that means going on that cruise you promised your spouse years ago. Or discovering America together in an RV. Or playing all your dream golf courses. Or finally starting that pottery business with your husband.

Whatever those things are, those are the items on your retirement "bucket list." Everybody's bucket list is different. When I sit down with retirees, I generally hear bucket list items such as Europe, an African Safari, traveling with family, Asia, Australia, New Zealand, Alaska, cruises, famous U.S. Parks, and more... Amazing places to visit and experience.

Your Bucket List "Window of Opportunity:" Three Crucial Ingredients of Your Bucket List Window

As someone who's worked with many retirees since starting in the financial services industry in 1994 as an insurance professional, I've got one crucial piece of advice: Don't put it off. Get to it now. Whatever is on your "bucket list," get to it early in retirement. Here's why: If you're like most retirees, you're going to be in your best health early on in your first years after retirement. I wrote on Kiplinger about taking advantage of your first 10 years of retirement which I call your "Go-Go Years".[61]

---

[61] Craig Kirsner. Kiplinger.com. February 25, 2022. "Retirees: Go Ahead and Spend More in the Go-Go Years."
https://www.kiplinger.com/article/retirement/t062-c032-s014-retirees-go-ahead-and-spend-more-in-go-go-years.html

Early in your retirement is when you're most likely to have these three necessary elements going for you _at the same time_:
- ✓ **Money**
- ✓ **Health**
- ✓ **Time**

You only have a limited window when you will have all three elements in place at the same time... And none of us knows how long that window will be open for them:

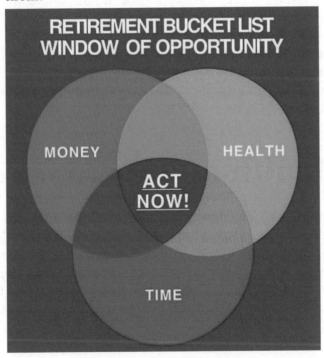

Money: There are 4 phases

Most of my clients are retired millionaires. So the 'money' part of the equation is usually manageable, given proper planning and risk management.

Our goal is to help keep their money window open for a long time, sometimes for multiple generations. If you're starting out with a big enough retirement portfolio, the money factor is usually manageable. At least it is for my retired millionaire clients.
So it's important to set up a retirement plan designed to help mitigate losses – you often "win" by not losing! <u>Warren Buffet</u> is famous for saying a lot of things, but his top 2 rules of investing are: <u>Rule #1: Never lose money. Rule #2: Never forget rule No.1.</u>[62] The other two vital items to accomplish your bucket list are closely interrelated: Your *health*, and your *time.*

Health: Don't Let Inertia Set In

As we get older, many of us begin to lose endurance and mobility. It gets harder to keep up with the grandchildren.
What's more, the grandchildren get older, too. And more independent. They'll have less and less time for you. They'll be dating and borrowing the car and

---

[62] Phil Town. RuleOneInvesting.com. December 22, 2022. "102 Warren Buffett Quotes on Life, Success, & More."
https://www.ruleoneinvesting.com/blog/how-to-invest/warren-buffett-quotes-on-investing-success/

working jobs or going to college – just as you did when you were their age!

Later in life, you may have other demands on your time. There may come a time when you have medical appointments multiple days a week which might put a crimp in your travel plans.

At a certain point, some of those bucket list activities that you've always wanted to do with your family, friends, and loved ones may not be an option for you anymore... This is not to be a downer, retirement can and should be a joyous time. But don't let time get away from you. Many people take it easy for a while, and then inertia may set in. Some retirees settle into a routine, continually putting off those important bucket list tasks for one reason or another.

Another day becomes another month. A month becomes a year. And then their health might fail. Or their time runs out altogether. It's better to pass away tired than pass away with regrets at the things you didn't get around to doing.

Time: What to do Now

First, preserve your health: stay *active*. There are no guarantees when it comes to personal health. But your chances at having a long and healthy retirement, with a lot of mobility and energy to take on those bucket list tasks are a lot better if you get off the couch!

Studies have shown that 20 years of a sedentary lifestyle <u>means twice the risk of a premature death</u>

<u>compared to being physically active.</u>[63]

The same study also found that people who became active later in life could mitigate the damage done even by many years of a sedentary lifestyle.

There's a great book called <u>The Grace to Race</u> which is about a nun who never exercised until almost turning age 50 when she started running... and now she still runs marathons at her age 80! I'm not recommending you run a marathon (I only run about 2 miles followed by kickboxing and weights three days a week) but the point is that it's never too late to start an exercise routine.

And it's not just a matter of longevity - it's also a matter of quality of life! A sedentary lifestyle is strongly correlated with earlier onset of strokes, diabetes, heart disease, and dementia.

The more physically active you are over a period of years the more time you're likely to have for your bucket list. Staying active throughout your retirement goes a long way to helping keep your money-health-time window of opportunity open for many years.

So buy that cruise ticket. Fly somewhere and rent that RV. Take the grandchildren to Disney. Take your family to see your favorite sports team in the playoffs. You might not get another chance!

Whatever's on your bucket list, start doing it *today!* Because tomorrow is not promised so just do it!

---

[63] Alisa Hrustic and Emilia Benton. MensHealth.com. October 31, 2022. "7 Surprising Ways You Wreck Your Body When You Don't Get Off Your Butt."
https://www.menshealth.com/health/g19541989/effects-of-sedentary-lifestyle/

CHAPTER TWENTY-NINE

The Myth That You Should Always be Fully Invested in the Market

This chapter might alternately be titled, "Is the 'Buy-and-Hold Best Days' Argument Fact or Fiction?"

Buy-and-hold proponents frequently cite the "best days" argument in support of the buy-and-hold strategy. They produce statistics intended to show that a large portion of the stock market's total gains are contained in only a handful of days – the "best 10," "best 25," the "best 100" etc. Therefore, the argument goes, investors must stay invested at all times for fear of missing those "best days."

A look at the 20 years of data from January 1, 2000, to December 31, 2019, however, reveals what I believe are significant flaws in the "best days" argument:

1) The 100 best days in the market are completely offset by the 100 worst days (plus 382.2% for the best days versus minus 383.7% for the worst days). "Best days" and "worst days" historically have occurred at about the same frequency and at about

the same size — interestingly, they were almost the mirror image of one another.

2) You can't be in the market to get the benefit of the 100 best days without being in the market and feeling the damage from the 100 worst days. The ups and downs could potentially net you nothing.

3) It is a well-documented fact that bear markets are characterized by substantially higher volatility than bull markets. Therefore, one might expect that more of the "best" and "worst" days would occur in bear markets than in bull markets. But the degree of lopsided-ness is surprising:

Best 100 Days (January 1, 2000 – December 31, 2019):

10 of the top 10 occurred in <u>Bear</u> markets (100%)
20 of the top 25 occurred in <u>Bear</u> markets (80%)
43 of the top 50 occurred in <u>Bear</u> markets (86%)
69 of the top 100 occurred in <u>Bear</u> markets (69%)

Worst 100 Days (Jan. 1, 2000 – Dec. 31, 2019):

8 of the top 10 occurred in <u>Bear</u> markets (80%)
20 of the top 25 occurred in <u>Bear</u> markets (80%)
37 of the top 50 occurred in <u>Bear</u> markets (74%)
66 of the top 100 occurred in <u>Bear</u> markets (66%)

So, in the past the best and worst days were not only more likely to occur during bear markets than during bull markets, but they occurred significantly more during bear markets.

4) Therefore, supporters of the "best days" argument are in effect saying that in order to get the benefit of the best days, you must be fully invested during

bear markets, because that's when most best days have occurred.

However, not only could you end up with nothing in the above example since the "best 100 days" are essentially offset by the "worst 100 days" — actually you could even end up with less than nothing, since the bear markets during this time took away a good 50% of your money — while you were hanging around waiting for those "best days" —twice!

A later chapter presents charts detailing "The 100 Best and Worst Market Days" for the S&P 500 from Jan. 1, 2000, through Dec. 31, 2019. The research was provided by W.E. Sherman and Co., LLC, and reprinted with permission.

Conclusion:

The "best days" argument is both misleading and potentially damaging to investors and retirees, in my opinion. It really ignores the potentially offsetting "worst days," and it doesn't recognize that the overwhelming majority of "best days" that can occur during bear markets.

So, is it fact or fiction? I would have to say ... **Fiction**.

Wouldn't it be better to simply try to help skip the bear markets altogether and leave all those "best days" to somebody else?

In our view, yes!

CHAPTER THIRTY

Special Report: Are Blue-Chip, Dividend-Paying Stocks Really "Safe?"

As seen on Kiplinger[64]

Four examples of why even well-known companies aren't always worth the investment

For many investors — newbies and veterans alike — there is often an attraction to big corporations. If a company is a household name (and you perhaps even have some of their products in your house), this might appear to be a relatively "safe" investment.

And because many of these blue-chip stocks usually pay dividends, this seems like a win-win situation, especially for retired investors who depend on income. But, as recent history shows, this isn't always the best idea.

---

[64] Media appearances were obtained through a PR program. The media outlets were not compensated in any way.

What Is a blue-chip stock exactly?

In order to be considered a blue-chip stock, a company has to have been in business for a long time with billions in market capitalization. This type of company is typically one of the leaders in its industry.

Examples include Disney, IBM, and Coca-Cola. And, as mentioned, these companies often issue dividends to shareholders on a quarterly and sometimes annual basis.

Why shouldn't all of these top global companies be considered rock-solid investments?

Often, there's no such thing as a good stock in a bad market.

When things are going well, blue-chip stocks can seem like a stable way to realize market gains. A strong economy generally results in consumers buying from these companies, which maintains — or raises — the stock price and allows investors to keep getting their nice dividends.

But what happens when things stop going so well?

There's a perception that these well-established corporations will stay strong even during bad markets. But this often just isn't true, as evidenced by General Electric's downturn during the Great Recession. In 2008, GE's quarterly dividend was 30 cents per share. When the worldwide recession hit, that dropped to 10 cents during 2009's second quarter.[65]

---

[65] Sarah Hansen. Investopedia. Updated May 5, 2022. What Happens to Dividends During Recessions and Bear Markets? https://www.investopedia.com/insights/rise-and-fall-ge/

The fact is that in 2009 about 1/3 of companies that paid dividends cut them or stopped paying them entirely.[66]

But that wasn't the full story on GE's disastrous troubles. This massive company, a historic high-flyer in the market, has been plagued by debt, much of it from unfunded pension plans and a series of poor management decisions.

GE lost over $140 billion in market value in 2017 alone, causing it to be kicked out of the venerable Dow Jones Industrial Average — the index that tracks the bluest of the blue-chip companies.[67] The share price of GE has dropped by over 80% in the past twenty years.[68]

Poor foresight

AT&T is another example of a blue-chip stock that has struggled mightily in recent years. One reason cited for this is the company's reliance on its pay TV business, while more and more consumers are cutting cords.[69]

In a period of over four years, AT&T lost more than 9.5 million customers from its Premium TV Services division.

---

[66] simplysafedividends.com. 2023."What Happens to Dividends During Recessions and Bear Markets?"
https://www.simplysafedividends.com/world-of-dividends/posts/1038-what-happens-to-dividends-during-recessions-and-bear-markets

[67] Sarah Hansen. Investopedia. May 5, 2022. "The Rise and Fall of General Electric (GE)"
https://www.investopedia.com/insights/rise-and-fall-ge/ [67]

[68] Yahoo Finance. December 31, 2022.
finance.yahoo.com/quote/GE?p=GE&.tsrc=fin-srch

[69] Jon Brodkin, Arstechnica.com. August 3, 2021. "Awful transaction and timing: AT&T financially ditches DirectTV."
https://artstechnica.com/information-technology/2021/08/att-completes-directv-spinoff-after-6-years-of-utter-failure-and-ineptitude/

In the past five years alone, the value of AT&T shares has dropped 44%.[70]

Fluctuating prices

Companies that make things often have to rely on procuring the right elements to create their products. For instance, without cocoa, Hershey wouldn't be able to make the vast majority of its food items. And when cocoa prices increased to more than $3,000 per metric ton in 2015, this hurt Hershey significantly.[71]

Hershey's stock price was $31.99 on March 6, 2009, and recently hit an all-time high of $262.70 on June 16, 2023. [72]

Lack of Innovation

Corporations can't stand on name recognition alone. Proctor & Gamble is the maker of Tide, Crest, Charmin, and many other products.

From 2013 to 2018, the overall price of the stock fluctuated between a high of $93.46 on December 26, 2014, and a low of $68.42 on September 11, 2015. That's a downturn of almost 27%. Since Covid, the stock has risen to $155 a share as of May 5, 2023.[73]

---

[70] Yahoo Finance. December 31, 2022. finance.yahoo.com/quote/T?p=T&.tsrc=fin-srch

[71] James Brumley. InvestorPlace. April 18, 2018. "Hershey Co. Has Become a Molten, Gooey Mess."
https://investorplace.com/2018/04/hershey-co-hsy-stock-molten-gooey-mess/

[72] Yahoo Finance. Accessed June 16, 2023. finance.yahoo.com/quote/HSY?p=HSY&.tsrc=fin-srch

[73] Yahoo Finance. May 5, 2023. finance.yahoo.com/quote/PG?p=PG&.tsrc=fin-srch

Why diversification is the key

There is certainly nothing wrong with investing in blue-chip stocks, but you know what they say about putting all of your eggs in one basket. This is why one of the smartest things investors — and particularly retired investors — can do is diversify their portfolios to include fewer volatile investments.

At Kirsner Wealth Management, we can help you do this. We focus on diversification for our clients, including more diversified investments such as institutional mutual funds and ETFs and more conservative investments designed to help preserve your wealth. In addition, we utilize software to analyze portfolios and assign a Risk Number from 1 to 99, followed by rebalancing investments to hit your personalized Risk Number.

CHAPTER THIRTY-ONE

7 Myths About Variable Annuities:
Exposing Their Dark Side

As seen on Kiplinger[74]

On the surface, variable annuities sound almost too good to be true. But once you learn the facts about the protection of your principal, the fees and how the income is paid out, you'll see they might not be as great as they sound for retirees.

By Craig Kirsner, MBA

One of the most misunderstood investment strategies I've come across since 1994 is the variable annuity. When I audit existing variable annuities, I get the facts about them by calling the insurance company directly rather than the broker who sold them. Why? Because I believe you should trust but verify, and I like to get my information directly from the horse's mouth.

---

[74] Media appearances were obtained through a PR program. The media outlets were not compensated in any way.

When I call the insurance company, among other questions, I ask: What are all the fees? What is the risk? What are the features? After going through that drill numerous times, I've pretty much seen it all. Based on my experiences over the past 29 years, the following are the seven most common myths I've learned about variable annuities and the facts dispelling those myths:

Myth #1: A variable annuity is a suitable investment for a retiree

I typically work with high-net worth clients, but regardless of your means, your **investing goals and strategies evolve as you grow older.**

Early in life, you were probably happy to ride with the ebb and flow of the market, waiting and hoping to hit that investment "home run." And why not? Suffering a loss now and then didn't bother you because your confidence for a rebound, and you knew you had plenty of time to recover, long before retirement.

But years pass and investing approaches change. Entering retirement, most people start thinking about protecting and preserving what they have, not making a big splash in the market.

You may have heard it said that these days the return OF your principal is more important than the return ON your principal, and that is definitely true for most of our clients. That's why the variable annuities some retirees count on for a regular income may not be the best route to take. Which brings us directly to Myth #2.

<u>Myth #2</u>: **Your money is safe**

People are often led to believe by their brokers that with variable annuities their money is safe, which couldn't be further from the truth. Your money is typically invested in underlying mutual funds which are called investment options or variable investment options, with no real protection of your principal.

The name of the annuity pretty much sums it up: "Variable," as in the principal varies, unlike a fixed annuity, where the principal is guaranteed by the insurance company and backed by their financial strength and claims paying ability.

In a variable annuity, your cash value is determined by how well your selected mutual fund options perform, meaning it generally depends on the whims of the market. Some variable annuities offer optional riders that you can purchase for an added fee to provide a level of guarantee to your annuity values or your potential income stream. But without these, your annuity no offers guarantees to your principal.

Here's an eye-opening exercise: Call your variable annuity insurance company's customer service line and ask the representative what the cash value of your annuity was on October 12, 2007, and what it was worth on March 6, 2009. This shows you your values using the top of the market to the bottom of the market. Then you will know exactly how much you may have lost during the last major crash, and more importantly how much it has grown since March 2009. Hopefully you are well ahead of where you were in 2007 before the last crash, or at least breaking even at this point.

What if you purchased your variable annuity after 2009, and you enjoyed the bull market we had for over a decade since then? In that case, ask the insurance company what the value of your annuity was on February 19, 2020, and then again on March 23, 2020. This will show you how much you might have lost in that six-week COVID crash, which will give you an idea of how at-risk your principal is.

Albert Einstein is credited with saying, "The definition of insanity is doing the same thing over and over again and expecting a different result." If your goals and needs have changed now that you are in retirement and are more concerned with preserving and protecting your wealth and keeping your fees low, then it might be a good time to change your retirement strategy to match your goals and needs.

<u>Myth #3</u>: Your fees are low

Variable annuities typically have high, often hard to find or understand fees — which can range from 2% to 4% per year — that can eat away at your money, potentially leaving little to nothing for your beneficiaries and really dragging on your overall investment performance. [75]

Variable annuities typically have up to five different fees! Again, you can call your variable annuity customer service line to ask what your specific fees are, which might include: [76]

---

[75] Dana Anspach. TheBalanceMoney.com. November 26, 2021. "5 Variable Annuity Fees to Ask About."
https://www.thebalancemoney.com/variable-annuity-fees-to-ask-about-2389027
[76] Dana Anspach. TheBalanceMoney.com. November 26, 2021. "5 Variable Annuity Fees to Ask About."
https://www.thebalancemoney.com/variable-annuity-fees-to-ask-about-2389027

Fee #1: Mortality and Expense (M&E) Fee
Fee #2: Administration or Distribution Charge
Fee #3: Mutual Fund Manager Expense (typically averages about 1%)
Fee #4: Income Rider Fee, if applicable
Fee #5: Death Benefit Rider Fee, if applicable

That's a lot of fees! I have seen 4% annual fees on a regular basis in variable annuities that I review for clients in my financial planning practice.

Myth #4: Your income rider value is your cash value

I have heard many clients say the broker told them money in a variable annuity is safe and can't be lost. As I proved above, that's just not the case because your cash value goes up and down based on the mutual fund options you're invested in, minus the annual fees in the variable annuity.

What your broker is generally referring to is the addition of an income rider, which might grow at, let's say, a hypothetical 6% a year. Some people believe they are earning 6% on their money, and that they can walk away with this lump sum 6% growth in the future. This couldn't be further from the truth! If you think it about it logically, for the insurance company to pay you a 6% annual return, they would have to be earning approximately 9% a year to be able to pay you 6% and pay the broker a commission and still make a profit. Insurance companies typically earn closer to 4.1% per year because, by law, they must invest very conservatively in mostly corporate bonds and some real estate. So, it just isn't possible for them to pay you 6% and still have <u>a profitable product</u>[77]

What this really means is that only your income rider is growing at 6% per year, and if you want to walk away in the future with a lump sum of money, you aren't getting the 6% per year growth income rider value. Instead, you will walk away with whatever your cash accumulation value is based on your investment option results, less the annual fees you paid each and every year.

The 6% rider only says that at some point in the future you can turn on a guaranteed income stream (which reflects a 6% increase each year) for life and that if you outlive your money, the insurance company will continue to pay you that income for as long as you live. Sound good? Sure. But wait until you read the rest of the story…

Myth #5: Your income rider is an efficient way to receive income for life

Let me explain how an income rider really works using a hypothetical scenario. Let's say you buy a variable annuity at age 65 from an insurance company for $1 million, and they might pay you an income stream of 5% per year for life, or $50,000 per year for as long as you live starting immediately.

The good news is that this is a income for life, so even if you run out of money in the account, the insurance company will still pay you $50,000 per year for as long as you live. The bad news is that the $50,000 they are giving

---

[77] National Association of Insurance Commissioners U.S. Life and Health Insurance Industry Analysis Report for year end 2021, https://content.naic.org/sites/default/files/inline-files/2021%20Life%20Annual%20Industry%20Commentary.pdf

you comes out of your own $1 million, until this amount is gone. So, they are giving you your own money back!

What's worse is that if your fees total 4% per year, or $40,000 in this case, they are charging you $40,000 per year to give you $50,000 of your own money. I don't think it's efficient to pay someone $40,000 per year for them to give you $50,000 of your own money, but that's how this product typically works. Of course, there may be years in which your investment options provide nice returns and this can help increase the amount of your annual payout to be greater than $50,000 – but you're also subjecting your money to market volatility and it can also go down in value.

The really bad news is that, assuming no added gains to your annuity, if they are withdrawing $50,000 of your funds from your account (5%) and charging you $40,000 in fees (4%), that means each year your annuity value is going going down by $90,000 or 9%! You must earn 9% per year just to have your cash value stay the same!

Now, you might have heard about the 4% withdrawal rule, which analysts at Morningstar recently lowered to 3.3% This rule of thumb states that you should take about 3.3% of your account value out each year to expect your retirement nest egg to last, assuming a balanced portfolio, fixed real withdrawals over a 30-year time horizon, and a 90% probability of success. Clearly, taking 9% out of a volatile asset like a variable annuity might be difficult to achieve going forward. [78] [79]

Lastly, what happens if you have one or two bad years in the market and your principal potentially loses up to 50%, going down to $500,000? The insurance company will still pay you $50,000 out of your money, and your fees might still be approximately $20,000. That means your annuity value is now going down by $80,000 out of your $500,000 each year, or 16% of your principal! It's really challenging to have your money grow if you are taking 16% per year out of your money.

Myth #6: Your lifetime income will go up after you turn it on

Your adviser might have told you that your income could go up after you turn it on. Perhaps you looked at an illustration that showed if you bought the variable annuity in 1995 and immediately turned on your income, that income would have increased during that incredible bull market from 1995 to 2001.

But here's the rest of the story: The only way to increase your income payout is if the market consistently earns more than the 9% your annuity value is decreasing each year in income and fees. While it's possible that you might

---

[78] Reshma Kapadia. Barrons.com. Dec. 14, 2021. "Forget the 4% Rule. Why Retirees Need to Rethink Their Withdrawal Strategy." https://www.barrons.com/articles/retirement-withdrawal-strategy-4-percent-rule-51639177201

[79] Christine Benz and John Rekenthaler. Morningstar.com. Nov. 11, 2021. "What's a Safe Retirement Spending Rate for the Decades Ahead?" https://www.morningstar.com/articles/1066569/whats-a-safe-retirement-spending-rate-for-the-decades-ahead

earn more than 9% year every year out without having a losing year in the market, the odds are that starting from where we are in the stock market in early-2023, it's not very likely that you can count on consistently earning more than 9% per year without experiencing a down year.

Because of those facts, it's much more likely there will be no income increase for inflation in the future because you can't really count on earning significantly more than 9% year in and year out. So, what will $50,000 of income actually buy in 10 or 20 years?

<u>Myth #7</u>: Your family will always get the death benefit

Many people I come across have a death benefit rider, and they are under the impression their family will always receive the death benefit as a lump sum. But that often isn't the case.

As we discussed above, reducing your annuity's value by 9% per year means that at some point during your life you have a greater chance to run out of money in your account.

If you run out of money in your contract, the insurance company annuitizes the income rider value, which means they will continue to pay the $50,000 income to you, but the day you die, your family will no longer receive a lump sum death benefit.

This makes common sense... The insurance company can't afford to give you $50,000 per year for as long as you live and pay your entire $1 million back to your beneficiaries if there is no money left in your account, right?

Some brokers have told my clients to just stop taking the $50,000 yearly income when the account reaches $1,000 in cash value to preserve the lump sum death benefit for their family. The problem with that idea is that the fees at that point might still be significant each year. That's because the insurance company charges their rider fees based upon the income rider value and the death benefit rider value, which might still be a $1 million rider value!

And many retirees wouldn't want to stop taking $50,000 per year in income they live on to all of a sudden pay thousands per year to cover those rider fees! It's just often not feasible.

So now that I've explained the seven common myths about variable annuities and you have learned the facts about them, you can see why I generally don't think they are a good option for a retiree – whether you're a high-net worth client like the ones I meet with, who have over $1 million in investable assets, or someone with more modest savings to preserve. Retirement is the time to reap the benefits of your hard work. This not the time to take big risks, because in retirement, if you're not careful you can deplete your savings pretty quickly.

Our clients are looking to help preserve their wealth and leave a legacy to their family, and I believe that variable annuities aren't in line with those goals.

To watch our full video about Variable Annuities from Craig Kirsner, MBA, go to Kirsner Wealth Management's YouTube channel.

Section 3:

Strategic IRA and Tax Planning Strategies for Millionaires, and the "Elimination" of the Stretch IRA

CHAPTER THIRTY-TWO

Income Taxes and the "Elimination" of the Stretch IRA

United States Judge Billings Learned Hand was famous for saying:

"Any one may so arrange his affairs that his taxes shall be as low as possible; he is not bound to choose that pattern which will best pay the Treasury; there is not even a patriotic duty to increase one's taxes."

I don't know about you, I don't mind paying my fair share of taxes, I just don't want to pay any more!

While not many of us are the biggest fans of taxes, we do appreciate all the things that those taxes pay for.

Roads, bridges, schools, and much more. It is the patriotic duty of every American to pay their fair share of taxes. Many would agree with me. Yet, while they don't mind paying their fair share, they're not interested in paying 1 cent more!

This is especially important because we know that the current tax cuts are set to expire after 2025! [80] So if the government doesn't do anything, taxes will be higher in a few years so we believe you should be doing proactive tax planning especially if you have a substantial IRA accumulation. This is because your IRA might be what I call a "ticking tax time bomb"... and it's either pay taxes now or pay taxes later. Someone is going to pay taxes so my clients want to attempt to pay as little as possible over their lifetimes.

Now, the mere mention of taxes probably takes your mind to the April 15th tax season. You are probably filled with dread when you think about everything you have to do to prepare... The forms, the accountant meetings, the W-2 forms you get in the mail.

Let's face it: the mere thought of taxes might set some people into a frenzy. It's almost never a pleasant thing to talk about. That's partly why they're so important, however.

So many of the clients that come into my office tell me that they never consult with their accountant except during tax season. Their tax professional, therefore, maybe isn't really doing all he or she could do for you. I recommend you change your relationship with your current accountant or get a new one, someone who can be there as your all-around tax planner.

What's the difference between a tax professional and a tax planner? Tax planning is something that goes beyond tax season. Your tax planner will work with you year-round to help you maximize your dollar and keep as much of your money as possible in your pocket.

---

[80] Amy Fontinelle. Investopedia.com. Dec 27, 2022. "How the TCJA Tax Law Affects Your Personal Finances."
https://www.investopedia.com/taxes/how-gop-tax-bill-affects-you/

Now, as a caveat, I want to emphasize that I am not an accountant, however, we do have a tax planning software called Holistiplan that allows us to help accountants do proactive tax planning for our clients. I see the way taxes affect my clients, and I have plenty of experience helping clients with tax-efficient strategies in their retirement plans in conjunction with their tax professionals.

We have strategic partnerships with several different accountants in the area. They can help our clients minimize their taxes as much as possible.

It's especially important to me to help my clients develop tax-efficient strategies in their retirement plans. Each dollar they retain is a dollar we can put to work. Income tax planning is important.

The current U.S. debt level is $31 trillion and growing fast![81] As a result, the government needs tax revenue!

The government passed the SECURE Act starting in 2020 which effectively ended the stretch IRA concept for most non-spouse beneficiaries, as we discuss in the following slides from my seminar ...

The "Elimination" of the STRETCH IRA!

Since 2020, when you leave your IRA to your children after you're gone, for the majority of them they won't be able to do a stretch IRA.

They will have to withdraw all of your IRA money over only ten years after your death!

---

[81] U.S. Debt Clock. 2023. https://usdebtclock.org

We have a number of strategies to help deal with the elimination of the stretch IRA for non-spouse beneficiaries which we can discuss at our meeting.

Here's one potential strategy to deal with IRAs now...

If you were a farmer,
Would you rather pay taxes on your penny seeds or million-dollar harvest?

$1M

1¢

Clearly, if you were a farmer, you'd rather pay taxes on the seeds, not the eight-foot-tall wheat. Most people would rather pay taxes on the pennies, not the dollars and that's why a Roth IRA could be a powerful strategy, especially with the elimination of the Stretch IRA!

We call this our S.R.I. plan, which is our <u>Strategic Roth Integration</u> plan. This way you're taking advantage of your current tax brackets and choosing to pay taxes now rather than later.

For example, let's say someone owns Apple stock in their IRA and Apple took a big hit in 2022, dropping 27%! So at the end of 2022, they did a partial Roth IRA conversion and moved $50,000 of that beaten up Apple stock to their Roth IRA. They paid income taxes on the $50,000. However if Apple goes up in the future then all the gains on that Apple stock are now tax-free! So he took advantage of Apple's stock lower prices to do the Roth IRA conversion, and if it goes up all the future growth on that $50,000 of stock is now tax-free (assuming withdrawals are after age 59-1/2 and the Roth account has been open for at least 5 years)! [82] Market volatility can be a potentially great tool for proactive financial planners to take advantage of lower stock prices for Roth IRA conversion opportunities.

The Fed

In the United States, taxes can be a rather uncertain proposition. This is especially true with the national debt being so high. According to USDebtClock.org, we have over $31 trillion in debt!

I'm not trying to freak you out or anything. Chances are, you've had an idea about this debt for a long time. My point is, even though our personal income taxes aren't terrible at the moment, we know taxes will be higher after 2025 and they could go even higher with our current debt situation. [83] In fact, as a higher net worth retiree, right now

---

[82] This is a hypothetical example provided for illustrative purposes only; it does not represent a real life scenario, and should not be construed as advice designed to meet the particular needs of an individual's situation.

[83] Amy Fontinelle. Investopedia.com. Dec 27, 2022. "How the TCJA Tax Law Affects Your Personal Finances." https://www.investopedia.com/taxes/how-gop-tax-bill-affects-you/

you might be in the lowest tax bracket you will have for the rest of your life!

So, you and the advisors working for you should always keep taxes in mind, and always try to reduce as much tax as possible for your situation. What are a few things we can do to reduce your overall tax bill? There are more ways than you might think.

Know Your Limits

One of the most important parts of tax planning is knowing what tax bracket you are in based on your income. Your income taxes are based on everything for which you owe taxes.

It's so important to know your tax bracket so you can do some planning... If you are in one tax bracket, how much more can you earn before you move up to the next bracket? You might find this knowledge especially helpful when making big financial decisions like giving an inheritance or rolling funds over from an IRA to a Roth IRA. A significant change in your income could affect your tax bracket position.

For instance, based on the 2023 tax table, John and Jane's taxable income of $371,200 puts them in the 32% tax bracket and $7,000 above the upper end of the 24% tax bracket. They have already maxed out their retirement funds' tax-exempt contributions for the year. Their daughter Susie is a sophomore in college. This couple may be able to shave $2,240 off their tax bill by using that $7,000 to reduce their taxable income by helping Susie out with groceries and school — something they were likely to do, anyway, but now can deliberately account for in their overall financial strategy.

Keep in mind this is only an example. Everyone's situation is different. But I hope you can see through this example just how important tax planning is in order to save yourself money.

Lower Tax Rate?

I have had many clients who simply assume they will be in a lower tax bracket as they approach retirement. If you think about it, their logic isn't wrong. Since you'll stop accumulating money from working and instead taking money out, you will have less income. Also, chances are, you won't have as many expenses as you once did.

The thing is, though, your overall lifestyle in retirement might not change much from when you were working. I haven't met many retirees who plan on travelling less or spending less money on their grandkids.

Chances are you might spend even more when you hit retirement, especially at the beginning when you are starting a new routine and spending a lot to enjoy the early years in retirement... in my Kiplinger article I named the first 10 years of retirement your "Go-Go Years". Sure, later on that may taper off, but usually just in time for their budget to be focused on health and long-term care expenses. Do you see where this is going? Many people plan as though their taxable income will be lower in retirement and are surprised when the tax bills come in and look the same as they used to. As my grandma always said, it's better to plan for the worst and hope for the best, wouldn't you agree?

401(k)/IRA

It's very possible that you'll need to keep track of how your 401(k) and IRAs perform, tax-wise, in retirement. It's likely you have one or more of these accounts, and hopefully you've diligently contributed a portion of each paycheck to these accounts. The thing is, though, all the funds you're contributing haven't broken away from the chains of taxes. Your funds might be tax-deferred, but certainly not tax-free. Unfortunately, nearly everything to do with money also has everything to do with taxes, including portions of our livelihood like the 401(k). Now that you're approaching retirement, those deferred taxes are now due to be paid.

Once these taxes are due — around age seventy-three, by the way — you're required to take out RMDs, or required minimum distributions. If you don't take out the RMD, you will be forced to pay a 25% tax penalty on the money you should have taken out (which can be further reduced to 10% if you correct it promptly). And that 25% tax doesn't count your income taxes owed.

Something you can do supplementally to your 401(k) is an account called a Roth IRA. These accounts are a way to save for your future self without paying taxes when withdrawing it in the future. Roth accounts are not tax deferred, so you pay the tax up front. Then when you eventually withdraw the funds, there are no taxes to pay. Roths also don't have RMDs, so you can keep the account growing even past the age of 73. The only thing to keep in mind, however, is that you must have owned the account for at least five years and take withdrawals after age $59\frac{1}{2}$ to receive all these benefits.

Keep all this in mind along with your tax bracket as you decide how you want to withdraw and distribute your retirement funds. Depending on who you are, how much money you have, and many other factors, it might be wise to convert your 401(k) or IRA to a Roth using our S.R.I. Strategic Roth Integration plan. Sometimes people take the funds from their RMDs and place them in other stock market investments or insurance products. You can find out these kinds of strategies — the kind that work in your favor — by consulting with a tax planner.

Tax Foundation.org recently provided the following updated income tax tables for 2023:[84]

Tax Rate	2023 Estimated Income Tax Brackets	
	Single Filers	Married filing jointly
10%	$0 to $11,000	$0 to $22,000
12%	$11,001 to $44,725	$22,001 to $89,450
22%	$44,726 to $95,375	$89,451 to $190,750
24%	$95,376 to $182,100	$190,751 to $364,200
32%	$182,101 to $231,250	$364,201 to $462,500
35%	$231,250 to $578,125	$462,501 to $693,750
37%	$578,126+	$693,751+

A single taxpayer has a $13,850 standard deduction and a married couple has a $27,700 standard deduction in 2023. Additionally, if you're over age 65 you can take an additional standard deduction of $1,500 per person for married couples and $1,850 if you're single. [85]

What does this mean to you?[86]

Now, I'm not an accountant, but it really irritates me when a client comes in and is proud that they pay almost

---

[84] Alex Durante. taxfoundation.org. "2023 Tax Brackets." Jan. 31, 2023. https://taxfoundation.org/2023-tax-brackets/

[85] Rocky Mengle. Kiplinger.com. "What's the Standard Deduction for 2022 vs. 2023?." Feb. 2, 2023. https://www.kiplinger.com/taxes/tax-deductions/602223/standard-deduction

[86] Kelly Phillips Erb. Forbes. Oct. 26, 2020. "IRS Announces 2021 Tax Rates, Standard Deduction Amounts And More."

no income taxes each year and then when I look at their portfolio they have significant IRA assets. Why does this bother me? Well, in 2023, a married couple that are both over age 65 can have approximately $120,150 in taxable income and still only be taxed in the 12% tax bracket! The $120,150 figure includes a $27,700 standard deduction, the $3,000 deduction for both being over age 65, in addition to $89,450 allowable in the chart above.

That is a significant potential tax planning opportunity to convert part of your IRA to a Roth IRA each year to take advantage of these very low, relatively speaking, tax rates. Then the growth on that Roth IRA is forever tax-free for you and your heirs! But your accountant may not be mentioning this opportunity to pay fewer income taxes, which is unfortunate in my opinion.

Let me give you a hypothetical example: if you're a married couple whose taxable income for 2023 is $60,150, and you converted an additional $60,000 of your IRA to Roth in 2023, on that $60,000 conversion you would pay approximately 12% or $7,200. Let's say that $60,000 in twenty years is worth $200,000 and you wanted to cash it in (after age 59-1/2 and the account is more than 5 years old)... you wouldn't pay one cent in taxes on that $140,000 of growth! In my opinion, that is a significant opportunity to pay $7,200 of taxes now than potentially substantially more in the future if the asset appreciates in value. [87]

Now, it is ideal when you convert to Roth you pay the $7,200 of income taxes with non-IRA assets like cash, so that you can let the entire $60,000 Roth IRA grow tax free

---

https://www.forbes.com/sites/kellyphillipserb/2020/10/26/irs-releases-2021-tax-rates-standard-deduction-amounts-and-more/?sh=6b05d8227b91

[87] This is a hypothetical example provided for illustrative purposes only; it does not represent a real life scenario, and should not be construed as advice designed to meet the particular needs of an individual's situation.

forever. If you can, don't remove IRA money to pay the $7,200 of taxes, use money from a non-IRA account to get the full benefit of the Roth.

By the way, this also applies to long term capital gains... In the above example you could realize $50,000 of long term capital gains and pay $0 income tax!!! Yes, $0 in taxes in that situation. A huge opportunity!

If you're like a large number of my retired millionaire clients whose taxable income is over $120,150, then the Roth IRA conversion might still make sense for 2 reasons: 1) what happens when one spouse dies and 2) the elimination of the stretch IRA for non-spouses:

1) When one spouse dies:

If you're a married couple you're now in a joint taxpayer bracket so for example if your taxable income is the same $120,150 we discussed above you're now in the 12% tax bracket as a married couple. However when one spouse dies, the surviving spouse (usually the wife) would jump up to be in the 22% tax bracket! And after the tax cuts expire in 2026 that tax bracket will be even higher! This is why the Roth IRA conversion could be important to consider for a surviving spouse to help keep their taxable income lower.

2) The elimination of the Stretch IRA for non-spouses:

When you die and leave your IRA to your children your children only have 10 years to empty your IRA completely. So lets assume the IRA you leave your children will earn 4% annual returns over the ten-year period after you leave the IRA to your children. This means that your children will have to take out approximately 14% of the IRA balance each and every year. This would allow them to take out the 4% annual yearly earnings along with 10% of the principal so the entire IRA is drained over that ten-year period without a potential big surprise tax hit in Year 10.

This 14% annual IRA withdrawal could put your heirs in a higher tax bracket. So for my clients, I think that choosing to pay a 24% income tax now might be a bargain compared to the potentially higher income tax brackets your heirs might have to deal with.

Additionally, if your children live in a state that has a state income tax, such as New York that has an 10.9% top state tax bracket, if you let your children pay the taxes after you're gone they might have to pay that additional 10.9% state income taxes on top of the federal income taxes.

We use a fantastic software call Holistiplan that helps you identify the maximum amount to withdraw year by year to take advantage of these current tax brackets, in conjunction with your accountant or a tax professional that we can refer to you.

Section 4:

Additional Advanced Retirement Planning Strategies for Millionaire Retirees

CHAPTER THIRTY-THREE

You Should Have a Personal Umbrella Liability Insurance Policy

Unfortunately, we live in a litigious society and the more money you have, the larger target you have on your back should a lawsuit of some sort arise.

To combat this, for example, a very wealthy individual that owns a large law firm might spend a tremendous amount of money each year legally transferring his assets to offshore trusts because he is afraid that he might be sued one day. This doesn't make those assets unreachable should he be sued. However, it does make those assets harder to find. Most of our clients want a simpler solution for asset protection...

One simple solution is a personal umbrella liability insurance policy that should help protect you financially if something bad happened and you get sued ... whether it's a car accident or someone slips and falls in your home, etc.

You can add a personal umbrella liability insurance policy onto your homeowner's insurance policy or your auto insurance policy. The best part is that $1 million of protection might only cost you about five hundred dollars per year... This is money well spent should a misfortune occur.

I heard of someone who was driving through an intersection on a Saturday night at 11 p.m. A teenager on a skateboard ran a red light. Unfortunately, the driver's vehicle hit the teenager, who later died. The driver didn't receive a ticket as it was clearly the teenager's fault. However, he was still sued and even though he was found to be only 5% at fault, this amounted to significant financial damages. Thankfully he had $2 million of liability insurance coverage which paid the claim. (He was also happy to own several guaranteed annuities. They are asset-protected in Florida, so if the $2 million of liability insurance wasn't enough, the lawsuit couldn't have taken his asset-protected annuity assets.)

Keep in mind that if you add this personal liability policy to your auto insurance policy, you might have to increase your auto insurance minimum coverage protection limits, which could increase your auto insurance premiums. However, my father-in-law has been an insurance adjuster for fifty years and he highly recommends having those higher auto insurance coverage limits anyway. It might be less expensive to add this umbrella policy to your homeowners insurance.

The general rule of thumb is the policy's protection should be at least $1 million or more ... ideally a minimum amount to cover your net worth, less your homes, IRAs, annuities, and life insurance cash value. Those assets are generally asset-protected anyway.

CHAPTER THIRTY-FOUR

What is Cryptocurrency and Blockchain?[88]

What is Cryptocurrency?

Even though 2022 was a horrible year for the performance of cryptocurrency, you should still know a bit about what it is and the future potential of this asset.

Just like the internet bubble of the 1990's burst in the early 2000's, 20 years later the internet is such a part of our lives that it's hard to think about our lives without it. That might be the same thing with cryptocurrency and blockchain technology over the next decade. So what is cryptocurrency?

Cryptocurrency, such as Bitcoin, is a digital currency. No bills to print for this currency... It is decentralized — there is no government, institution (like a bank), or other authority that controls it. Owners are anonymous; instead of using names, tax IDs, or Social Security numbers, cryptocurrency connects buyers and sellers through digital encryption keys. And it isn't issued from the top down, like an institution issues

---

[88] Neither AEWM nor advisors providing investment advisory services through AEWM recommend or facilitate the buying or selling of cryptocurrencies or blockchain.

traditional currency. Rather, cryptocurrency is "mined" by computers connected to the internet.

The value of Bitcoin is what people are willing to pay for it. This open market valuation also invites speculation (don't mortgage your house to buy cryptocurrency) and manipulation.

How can you buy cryptocurrency? If you're willing to assume the risk associated with owning cryptocurrency, there is an increasing number of digital currency exchanges like Kucoin and Coinbase — the largest and most established of them — where you can buy, sell, and store cryptocurrency. You can use cryptocurrency to buy things from online merchants, or just hang on to them.

There are more than 1,000 different coins out there, each with differing technologies behind them and you never know which will do well or which won't. It's like the early days of the internet, when many companies failed but many also did quite well. You can read the full article on what Bitcoin is at: https://www.nerdwallet.com/article/investing/what-is-bitcoin.

What Is Blockchain?

Blockchain is the invisible technology that's changing the world. Blockchain-based networks are becoming the foundation of much of your digital life. There's a new digital fabric remaking the internet beneath us, and you probably don't even realize it. Blockchain is a historical fabric underneath recording everything that happens on the internet — every digital transaction; exchange of value, goods and services; or private data — exactly as it occurs.

This technology has a myriad of potential uses for securely transferring data and digital assets over the internet. You can read the full article on what Blockchain is at:

https://www.nerdwallet.com/article/investing/blockchain

Both cryptocurrency and Blockchain are very risky, volatile investments. Make sure if you do invest a small portion of your retirement funds in it that you know the potential upside and downside of this technology.

CHAPTER THIRTY-FIVE

How Might Archegos' $10 Billion in Losses Affect Your Retirement?

Could derivatives cause the next financial crisis like they did in 2008? I'm seeing some very troubling signs.

As seen on Kiplinger, Nasdaq.com, Yahoo Finance and DailyRetirementNews.com by Craig Kirsner, MBA[89]

Imagine you walked into a Las Vegas casino and you brought <u>all</u> the money you had, let's say $1 million, and the casino gave you $105 million to gamble with. How smart do you think that would be for that casino? Well, as of March 31, 2023, Goldman Sachs Bank USA has 114 times their assets in total gross derivatives! [90] Credit default swaps were at the

---

[89] Media appearances were obtained through a PR program. The media outlets were not compensated in any way. Media outlets do not recommend or endorse the author or the content of this book.

[90] Office of the Comptroller of the Currency. First Quarter 2023. "Quarterly Report on Bank Trading and Derivative Activities." https://www.occ.gov/publications-and-

heart of the financial crisis in 2008 that caused the financial problems at AIG.[91] The insurance giant AIG had been selling credit default swaps for years, collecting small premiums, confident that the mortgage market wouldn't collapse, and that they'd never have to pay out a claim.

In 2008, the unthinkable happened: Mortgage markets collapsed — and mortgage lenders went to AIG expecting them to make good on their contracts. AIG didn't have the cash and couldn't raise it.

As of the first quarter of 2023, these are the 5 financial banks that are leveraging up with the most credit default swaps and similar derivative contracts which account for a whopping 95% of the total gross derivates contracts in the world!:[92]

Institution	Total Assets	Total Gross Derivatives (Notional)	Ratio
Goldman Sachs Bank USA	$490 Billion	$56 Trillion	114 to 1
Citibank National Assn	$1.7 trillion	$55 trillion	32 to 1

resources/publications/quarterly-report-on-bank-trading-and-derivatives-activities/files/q1-2023-derivatives-quarterly.html

[91] Robert McDonald. Kellogg Insight. Aug. 3, 2015. "What Went Wrong at AIG?" https://insight.kellogg.northwestern.edu/article/what-went-wrong-at-aig

[92] Office of the Comptroller of the Currency. First Quarter 2023. "Quarterly Report on Bank Trading and Derivative Activities." https://www.occ.gov/publications-and-resources/publications/quarterly-report-on-bank-trading-and-derivatives-activities/files/q1-2023-derivatives-quarterly.html

JP Morgan Chase Bank	$3.3 trillion	**$59 trillion**	<u>18 to 1</u>
Bank of America	$2.5 trillion	**$22 trillion**	<u>9 to 1</u>
Wells Fargo Bank	$1.7 trillion	**$13 trillion**	<u>7 to 1</u>

In 2021, non-regulated Archegos caused over $20 billion in losses

Archegos was set up as a family office, away from the oversight of the SEC.[93] As such they were allowed to take tremendous bets by using a derivative called a swap, which were bets on stocks using high leverage. Unfortunately, when those stocks went down, massive losses ensued. It is believed that Archegos had $10 billion in assets, yet was allowed to bet on $50 billion to $100 billion of stocks! 5 to 10 times leverage spread out among a number of banks that took losses during March of 2021.[94]

Even Goldman Sachs, which originally wouldn't do business with Archegos because the founder pleaded guilty to insider trading in 2012, changed their mind and thus was one of the banks that sold stocks in March 2021 to get out of those swap positions with Archegos. It's estimated that Archegos caused over $10 billion in losses at those banks, not to mention the tremendous drop certain stocks took when the stock selling occurred.

---

[93] Matthew Smith. Kiplinger. March 24, 2021. "Do I Need a Family Office? A Guide for the Rich and Not So Famous."
https://www.kiplinger.com/retirement/estate-planning/602492/do-i-need-a-family-office-a-guide-for-the-rich-and-not-so-famous

[94] Credit Bubble Bulletin. April 2, 2021. "Weekly Commentary: Archegos and Ponzi Finance."
https://creditbubblebulletin.blogspot.com/2021/04/weekly-commentary-archegos-and-ponzi.html

Derivatives Caused the Bankruptcy of Orange County, California, in 1994

This bankruptcy happened the way they always do: Slowly at first ... and then all at once. In 1994, Orange County, Calififornia suddenly went bankrupt. It was the biggest municipal bankruptcy in history at the time, and for almost two decades after that. [95] [96]

How did it happen? The county was struggling to fund basic services and was desperate to find ways to increase returns on its portfolio. Treasurer Robert Citron turned to derivatives — and massive amounts of leverage — for help to increase their returns.

The county got caught short when interest rates turned against them in 1994. When Wall Street refused to roll their short-term loans over, they were forced to realize the losses. The county lost over $1.6 billion much of it as a direct result of its ill-advised speculation in derivatives.[97]

Without access to credit markets, cities and local agencies might have trouble making their own obligations.

In 1998, just a few years later, we saw the spectacular collapse of Long-Term Capital Management — another massively leveraged project that speculated in derivatives.[98]

Fast forward to today.

---

[95] Eric Weiner. NPR. Feb. 28, 2008. "What Happens When City Hall Goes Bankrupt?"
https://www.npr.org/templates/story/story.php?storyId=60740288

[96] Alexander E.M. Hess, Michael B. Sauter and Samuel Weigley. Yahoo Finance. July 19, 2013. "The Largest Municipal Bankruptcies in U.S. History." https://finance.yahoo.com/news/largest-municipal-bankruptcies-u-history-214303904.html

[97] Teri Sforza. The Orange County Register. Dec. 6, 2019. "Here's how Oragne County went broke 25 years ago."
https://www.ocregister.com/2019/12/06/heres-how-orange-county-went-broke/

[98] Kimberly Amadeo. The Balance. Dec. 26, 2020. "Long-Term Capital Management Hedge Fund Crisis." https://www.thebalance.com/long-term-capital-crisis-3306240

Germany's financial giant Deutsche Bank is once again ramping up its exposure to a specific type of derivative called *credit default swaps* though the bank is currently looking to slowly unwind its exposure.[99] These contracts provide a ready way for lenders to insure themselves against the risk of default. But unless managed carefully, issuing or buying too many of these swaps can leave financial institutions dangerously overexposed to a sudden deterioration in the credit markets.

What's a Derivative?

A derivative is a financial instrument that derives its value from something else. There's no underlying asset — it's simply a contractual agreement for one party to pay to another in case something specific happens in the market.

In the case of a credit default swap, or CDS, lender A contracts with insurer B to pay money in the event their borrower C defaults.

CDS contracts basically function as insurance on bonds. A big lender might buy some CDSs to hedge its exposure, or to buy time for it to raise cash to cover the risk of a default. And a big insurance company or bank might sell CDS contracts to collect premium to goose its income and cash flow.

As long as the borrower C doesn't default, all is well.

Well, black swans (crazy events) occasionally happen. As discussed above, that's what happened to AIG. In 2008, AIG didn't have the cash and couldn't raise it.

That left banks and other mortgage lenders high and dry: If AIG couldn't honor their credit default swap contracts, they

---

[99] Mark DeCambre. Market Watch. July 28, 2019. "Deutsche Bank pegs its derivatives exposure at about $22 billion — and faces challenges in shedding those assets."
https://www.marketwatch.com/story/deutsche-bank-pegs-its-derivatives-exposure-at-about-22-billion-and-faces-challenges-in-shedding-those-assets-2019-07-26

didn't have the cash to keep operating. And everyone who relied on these banks was in trouble, too.

Berkshire Hathaway Chairman Warren Buffett said, "One of the lessons of the 2008-09 experience … was the fact that every company in the United States was a domino, and those dominoes were placed right next to each other. So when they started toppling, everything was in line."[100]

Buffett wisely declined to lend money to Lehman Brothers and AIG to keep them afloat during the crisis, in my opinion.

Money markets froze, as sellers of short-term commercial paper couldn't find buyers. Contagion threatened to cause a chain reaction that could bring down the economy as we knew it. It was only through concerted Fed and Treasury action that the U.S. was able to contain the damage.

Deutsche Bank pulled out of the derivatives business in 2014 after regulators drove up trading costs. But recent clearing technology innovations have substantially cut the cost of trading these contracts, making the business much more viable. As long as defaults are low, that is.[101]

How Widespread Is Derivatives Exposure?

Many banks have large derivative exposure so the risk is that the failure of one large buyer or seller of these contracts

---

[100] Nicole Friedman. Business Standard. Sept. 12, 2018. "Warren Buffett recounts his role during 2008 financial crisis." https://www.business-standard.com/article/international/warren-buffett-recounts-his-role-during-2008-financial-crisis-118090800809_1.html

[101] Christopher Whittall. Reuters. May 13, 2019. "New CDS nearly halves Deutsche Bank default projection costs." https://www.reuters.com/article/new-cds-nearly-halves-deutsche-bank-defa/new-cds-nearly-halves-deutsche-bank-default-protection-costs-idUSL5N22P2NV

could cause contagion: A rapid, cascading effect that could take down one financial giant after another in quick succession. In some worst-case scenarios, the chain reaction of failures could overwhelm central banks and their ability to hold back the damage.

Now, the good news is that these massive notional exposures are just that: Notional. You have to net out assets against liabilities: If you have $100,000 in the bank, and you owe a $100,000 loan, you don't have a notional exposure of $200,000. You have a net zero exposure.

Likewise with credit default swaps and other kinds of derivatives, you have to net the long positions against the short positions. According to the U.S. government, the fact is that the overall "net current credit exposure" is only $246 billion when they net out all of the derivatives among all of the U.S. institutions.[102] Not exactly chump change, but in theory, it's within the capacity of the capital markets to absorb.

That said, theory and reality are two different things... The risk of a general derivative-fueled crisis isn't so much because of the raw value of the exposure. The real risk is counterparty risk: Where one seller that didn't sufficiently balance its long and short positions gets caught in a cash crunch ... and cannot cover its promises to others.

Most institutions that get involved in derivatives look to balance out their exposure. They are both buyers and sellers of CDSs, looking for opportunities for price arbitrage, and finding ways to hedge their exposure by getting collateral from their counterparties.

AIG collapsed in 2008 because it didn't do this. It made the same mistakes in the 2000s that Orange County made in the 1990s. Instead of using CDSs as a *risk-reduction* tool as

---

[102] Office of the Comptroller of the Currency. First Quarter 2023. "Quarterly Report on Bank Trading and Derivative Activities." https://www.occ.gov/publications-and-resources/publications/quarterly-report-on-bank-trading-and-derivatives-activities/files/q1-2023-derivatives-quarterly.html

they were intended, it used them as a *speculative* one. In AIG's case, they always sold coverage, and never bought it.[103] After all, like any insurance contract, in order to earn the premium, all they had to do was provide a promise. It was free money — until the music stopped.

And when it stopped, AIG was caught with a pile of naked CDS promises it had sold that was worth <u>half a trillion dollars</u>: $300 billion to CDS buyers in the U.S. and $200 billion in Europe.

Goldman Sachs Bank USA will probably tell you not to worry because their "total credit exposure from all contracts" is only $76 billion when you net out the derivatives they hold with other banks.[104]

And they are correct that the risk isn't in the gross value — or even in the overall net exposure. Net exposures are not that high. <u>The real risks are as follows:</u>

💣 **Greed.** The temptation to speculate in these highly leveraged positions, rather than use them as risk management devices. It seems AIG may have gotten addicted to the small but steady stream of premiums that they mistook as profits, likely ignoring the risk of the massive liability accumulating on their books for years. And at Lehman Brothers, senior management started overruling risk management professionals.[105]

---

[103] Justin Fox. Time. Sept. 16, 2008. "Why the Government Wouldn't Let AIG Fail."
http://content.time.com/time/business/article/0,8599,1841699,00.html
[104] Office of the Comptroller of the Currency. First Quarter 2023. "Quarterly Report on Bank Trading and Derivative Activities."
https://www.occ.gov/publications-and-resources/publications/quarterly-report-on-bank-trading-and-derivatives-activities/files/q1-2023-derivatives-quarterly.html
[105] Navneet Arora, Priyank Gandhi and Francis A. Longstaff. January 2010. "Counterparty Credit Risk and the Credit Default Swap Market."
https://www.moodys.com/microsites/crc2010/papers/longstaff_counterparty.pdf

◆ **Incompetence.** The people running Orange County didn't mean to go bankrupt. They just didn't understand what they were getting into. And they dragged a number of cities and local pension funds with them.

◆ **The lure of false accounting.** Derivatives are complex— sometimes too complex for regulators and the investment community to understand, outside of a few specialists.

◆ **Counterparty risk.** See, it doesn't matter if you think your derivative position is totally balanced and nets out to zero. Because when you have a major bond issuer in your portfolio go belly up and you reach out to the next AIG, expecting them to wire the cash they promised, and they can't do it, you really weren't balanced at all. And when you fail, two of your own CDS buyers may be counting on you to meet your obligations the next day. And when you fail, they fail. But they have customers, too. And so on.

And then it might get worse. When every bank has a significant portfolio of derivatives without much transparency, and every bank has counterparty risk, no bank can risk doing business with any other. Which means the next time we have a major financial challenge, even a healthy bank might not want to buy the commercial paper from another bank, and this commercial paper market is what makes the entire financial world move.

When a crisis hits, things can get very ugly very fast. Like Orange County's bankruptcy, the crisis on Wall Street happened slowly at first — and then all at once. This is what Ben Bernanke and the Federal Reserve, Hank Paulson and the Treasury Department and President George Bush were facing over that fateful weekend in September of 2008 when they had to bail out the financial system.

So it's true on the surface theoretical level that it's not the gross exposure to credit default swaps that matters. It's the net exposure. But it's also true that if just one weak link in the chain happens to get caught short, like AIG, *it doesn't matter.* The rapid-fire chain reaction that can occur is unpredictable but could still be devastating — even if almost everybody thinks they did a good job netting out CDS sales and purchases.

The Bottom Line

No, you don't have to panic about the total notional value of the derivatives market. We aren't going to lose 10 times the total global economy.

But we could still see massive disruption, so diversification matters. And it's important to help protect yourself. At this time, if you are in or near retirement you might want to get a second opinion on your current retirement plan. Make sure you have the right investment mix for a diversified portfolio that has the right amount of risk for you.

CHAPTER THIRTY-SIX

Longevity

S ome might assume the scariest thing to a person over age sixty-five is the idea of death. As we age, it's natural to think that the grave will begin to be more frightening than anything. But something even scarier to most retirees is running out of money before they pass away.[106] This makes sense.... After all, most of us are living longer than ever before. The U.S. Census in 1950 indicated that life expectancy for a 65 year old was 78 for males and 81 for females. Nowadays, a 65 year old is expected to live to an average age of 83 if you're a male and 85 if you're a female![107]

Statistics reported by the Society of Actuaries show that for a married couple age 65 today, there is a 50% chance one of them will live to age 92![108]

---

[106] Jacques Buffett. Zety. Sept. 19, 2022. "More Frightening Than Death: Fear & Loathing in Retirement." https://zety.com/blog/afraid-of-retirement

[107] John Elflein. Statista. Oct. 25, 2022 "Life Expectancy – Men at the age of 65 years in the U.S." https://www.statista.com/statistics/266657/us-life-expectancy-for-men-aat-the-age-of-65-years-since-1960/

[108] Liz Weston. Tampa Bay Times. Nov. 9, 2020. "The financial upside to thinking about when you will die." https://www.tampabay.com/news/business/2020/11/09/the-financial-upside-to-thinking-about-when-you-will-die/

Unfortunately, however, many retirees haven't been planning for this boost in life expectancy. At your younger years, it probably wasn't your main priority to chuck money away into a retirement account even though you were probably planning to live to the ripe old age of 100.

It hits many people hard when they come closer and closer to retirement. They begin to see that their funds are finite. This limited amount of money paired with an upredictable lifespan can cause anxiety for retirees. Something else to consider as you age is healthcare. Unfortunately, there are many retirees that live longer but not healthier. Expenses for hospital, nursing home, and in-home care can be fairly high. A healthy 65 year old may ultimately spend more money on health care in the long run because they live longer.

As you can see, we can't have the best of both worlds in retirement: living longer doesn't necessarily mean living healthily. As we age, we will generally need more care. Think about paying the hefty price of chemotherapy or a pacemaker in your eighties, even if it's just deductibles and co-pays that you owe.

I know you're probably gaping at me right now, after pushing all this bad news on you.

I realize I've explained some dark stuff. But I promise, I'm merely concerned about the money side of things right now. It seems inhumane to calculate the price of a person, but it's simply something we have to do when considering longevity. It's common for people at age 45 and older to underestimate their lifespan by around 5 years or even more. Think about that. What if you planned to live until age 80 but you made it to 85? How will you support those 5 additional years of life if your money has run out?

It's never a bad thing to have a long life, but it comes at a cost. It's imperative that you plan in advance for it.

Long-Term Care

Living longer often goes hand-in-hand with the need for long-term care. Like many retirees, you probably mean to leave a legacy behind. If that's the case, it is so important find some way of paying for an extended stay in a long-term care facility. It's estimated that as many as 70% of all retirees will need some type of long-term care, so planning allows you to be safe rather than sorry.[109] Although this is an incredibly important thing to have in your golden years, the idea of long-term care sends too many retirees running in the opposite direction. Why? Because long-term care is one of the more stressful aspects of retirement planning that I deal with at my firm. It's very hard for aging people to consider a future in which they are physically and/or mentally limited, needing to be cared for often by other people.

I completely understand why many are hesitant to think about this kind of planning. But nevertheless, planning is the best way to feel any sense of relief!

Similar to the way you plan for and dream about your goals, it's also important to envision what you want your final decades on earth to look like. It's not going to be fun, but once you come to terms with the reality of the situation, I think it'll be worth it.

You might wonder what exactly I'm asking you to imagine. One thing to consider is your living situation. For example, how do you feel about leaving your house? It might be your main priority in retirement to stay in your house for as long as possible. If this is the case, you might want to consider home health care as an alternative to living in a nursing home.

---

[109] LongTermCare.gov. Accessed in 2023. "The Basics: How Much Care Will You Need?"
https://acl.gov/ltc/basic-needs/how-much-care-will-you-need

Perhaps you'll want to hire a professional, or maybe you have a friend or relative who is close by and willing to help you when you need it. If staying in your house isn't an option or even a priority, it might be time to have a conversation with loved ones about transferring to a retirement community. Perhaps you can live with a loved one as an alternative to assisted living.

All these options might be mind-boggling at first, but I promise it gets easier the more you think about it. It's so important to consider each possibility. The sooner you have a conversation with your loved ones, the better. Everyone around you will probably have questions and concerns that need to be answered right away. It's important to your family that they know your plans and wishes, even if it's difficult to talk about. It's also important to listen to what your spouse has to say. He or she may have different priorities or goals for their retirement.

It's completely natural for these conversations to be awkward and uncomfortable, especially when discussing matters with your children. It's important to explain to your children that they should really think things through before committing to caring for you in their old age. Often, young people impulsively agree to caring for their parents without knowing exactly how they would have to do it. This is a wonderful desire to have, but for working adults, it would be incredibly difficult to care for you full-time as well. Ask them to consider things more carefully. What would caring for you actually entail? Some might be able to handle doing the housework for you a few times a week, and some might be able to do even more. But ask them if they are prepared to go beyond basic tasks, like when you might need help going to the bathroom or bathing.

This isn't to say that I don't approve of families that take care of one another. In fact, I think it's a noble thing to be a part of when things run smoothly. But keep in mind the times that things might not work out. Many children of retirees dig themselves too deep into a hole that they won't be able to crawl back out of. And because these children promised to care for their ailing parents, there is no backing out. Things can become overwhelming or even toxic among family members that rely so heavily upon each other. If one begins suffering from a disease like Alzheimers, the condition can take a heavy toll on caretakers.

At the beginning, many don't know the realistic level at which they can help out other family members. Oftentimes, care takes more than one person to do correctly.

This is why it's so important to know what your specific retirement goals are. Once you've discussed things with your loved ones, you can use your goals as the base for conversation, thus planning for both best-case and worst-case scenarios.

Realistic Cost of Care

As you plan and discuss your goals, it's important to consider the true cost of long-term care. Many people underestimate just how expensive it can be.[110]

It's also important to consider inflation. Unfortunately for seniors, inflation, especially medical inflation, can negatively affect you. This inflation rate is one of the reasons why many don't estimate the cost of long-term care effectively.

Costs may change depending on where you live, but below is the national median for different types of long-term care.

---

[110] Brad Breeding. My Life Site. Aug. 10, 2020. "Many People Underestimate Their Future Cost of Care." https://mylifesite.net/blog/post/many-people-underestimate-their-future-cost-of-care/

This chart also takes inflation into account, which is illustrated by years.[111]

Average Long-Term Care Costs				
	Home Health Care, Homemaker Services	Adult Day Care	Assisted Living	Nursing Home (semi-private room)
Annual 2021	$59,488	$20,280	$54,000	$94,900
Annual 2031	$79,947	$27,255	$72,571	$127,538
Annual 2041	$107,442	$36,628	$97,530	$171,400
Annual 2051	$144,393	$49,225	$131,072	$230,347

Fund Your Long-Term Care

A big mistake I see often in my practice is when people don't plan for long-term care, assuming they will be covered by the government instead. They are completely wrong in thinking this. There are only two healthcare options the government offers: Medicare and Medicaid. I will say, these programs are often helpful to people in need of healthcare, but often there is no way either will adequately assist you in covering long-term care. Often, these programs will cover a portion of certain medical needs, but not everything. I don't

[111] Genworth Financial. Accessed 2023. "Genworth 2020 Cost of Care Survey." https://www.genworth.com/aging-and-you/finances/cost-of-care.html

necessarily know the entirety of these programs and their offerings, but I'll outline the basics below. If you want to know more details, you're always welcome to visit the websites Medicare.gov and Medicaid.gov.

Medicare

Medicare assists those who are over age sixty-five and those who are disabled. This program offers some nursing-home related are, but is limited. If they don't consider your nursing home stay to be a "custodial" or a long-term stay, things might be covered. For example, if you have a medical emergency like a heart attack and need to stay in a nursing home for rehabilitative care, you may be covered by Medicare. On the other hand, if you have a long-term illness like Alzheimers and cannot care for yourself adequately, then you won't be covered.[112]

Medicaid

Because Medicaid is administered differently from state to state, many rules regarding funding and protocol can change. Unlike Medicare, Medicaid is more likely to cover nursing home care, but it only supports retirees with low incomes.

Medicaid has an income limit, so if you are over that limit you'll have to use that income to pay for care. In your state, you will also be given a list of other things you can spend your assets on. This spending might include paying for your funeral, burial plot, or debts. Once you've done that, you will spend your money on nursing home care until it's all gone. Only after that will Medicaid will pay for the rest.

Many do not find this situation a problem because they think they can spend down their assets by giving early

---

[112] Medicare.gov. Accessed in 2023. "What Part A covers." https://www.medicare.gov/what-medicare-covers/part-a/what-part-a-covers.html

inheritances and monetary gifts. They think this will qualify them for Medicaid already. However, Uncle Sam thought this through already. Before you qualify for Medicaid, you must pass the rules of the "look-back" period, which is a test the government implements. They look at all the large purchases you made in the last five years, to make sure you haven't been heavily spending down your assets. After that, they decide if you've spent your money in the right places or not. If you gifted a little too much, you might not be eligible for Medicaid, even though you spent down your assets.

The idea of having even fewer retirement assets than you began with is scary. I say don't risk it. It's a much better option to save your money rather than relying solely on the government for your financial well-being.

Self-Funding

Some may want to pay for their retirement and healthcare expenses through self-funding. Using this method allows you to choose different kinds of products, each with different functions and personalities. For example, using your low-interest accounts may be a reliable way to save your money, but your income value will probably deplete as inflation rises. You also might be relying on high-interest assets like stocks and bonds, but it's always wise to consider what might happen in the long-term. It's possible that your assets might not hold out during volatile periods.

If you're considering self-funding, a lot of planning and wise decisions must be made. No matter what sort of product you want to invest in, there will always be some degree of risk. If your portfolio dwindles because of poor investment choices, retirement is the last place you want to be.

LTCI

Another option to consider when planning for long-term care is long-term care insurance (LTCI). Just like car or home insurance covers the expenses of those items, long-term care insurance assists you by covering the expense of long-term care. Their goal is to help preserve your assets while you have to spend time in a nursing home or in another facility.

Just like any other kind of insurance, a LTCI policy requires you to pay a monthly premium, which then enables the insurance company to cover you financially when you are in need of long-term care in the future. Oftentimes, policies cover an average length of stay, which is often around two or three years. According to the statistics, it's estimated that about 70% of Americans will be in a long-term care facility for around three years. But remember to not base your own situation on the average. About 20% of Americans will stay in long-term care for around five years. Plan for the worst situation, but hope for the best.[113]

Although LTCI can bring a lot of peace of mind, many reject it for certain reasons:

- Expense — As you've probably heard, long-term care can cost an arm and a leg. The younger you are, the less expensive it will probably be. To put things into perspective, let's consider a couple, each at age sixty. Let's assume that their long-term care insurance premiums will be around $2,010 per year for a basic three-year plan. As this couple gets older, their premium cost will gradually become larger.
- Limited options — LTCI isn't just expensive for you, it's can also be expensive for the companies that provide it. Because of this expense, fewer companies can afford to offer it. This small market of long-term care providers means that you have fewer options. Because you have

---

[113] LongTermCare.gov. Accessed in 2023. "The Basics: How Much Care Will You Need?" https://acl.gov/ltc/basic-needs/how-much-care-will-you-need

a unique set of circumstances, it's important to pick the best provider possible, but sometimes that provider isn't available because numbers are so few.

- Unavailability — LTCI is a lot like car insurance: the more wrecks you've been in, the harder it is to get insurance at all. With LTCI, the sicker or older you are, the less likely it is that you will qualify. Qualifying you for LTCI carries a large amount of risk for the insurance company; they often can't approve many people who will cost them thousands in bills.

- Potential loss— You might be someone who will never need long-term care. If you never have this need, you won't be able to take back the money you paid.

- Fluctuating rates — You might be paying $2,000 this year, but that rate is not fixed. Sometimes companies raise or lower the premium rates, which can cause seniors to make an impossible choice: continue a LTCI policy at a more expensive rate, or call it quits and lose your policy AND the money you've put into the policy so far.

Although only one in ten Americans aged fifty-five-plus have purchased LTCI, keep in mind the high cost of nursing home care. Can you afford $7,000 a month to put into nursing home care and still have enough left over to protect your legacy? This is a very real concern considering one set of statistics reported a two-in-three chance that a senior citizen will become physically or cognitively impaired in their lifetime.[114] So, not to sound like a broken record, but it is vitally important to have a plan in place to deal with longevity and long-term care if you intend to leave a financial legacy.

---

[114] payingforseniorcare.com. 2022. "Long-Term Senior Care Statistics" https://www.payingforseniorcare.com/statistics

If you are someone without it, ask yourself if you are able to pay $8,000 a month as a nursing home resident. Think about paying that for three or even five years. After your period of care, will you still have income left over? Will you still have enough to pass on an inheritance to your children? Sorry if I'm repeating myself, but as you hit retirement it's so important to have either LTCI, personal funds, or some other way of paying for long-term care.

Many of my clients don't buy LTC insurance because they have sufficient assets to "self-insure." Also, for many of my clients, if they did need long-term care they might actually spend less money because some expenses (for example, dining and travel) would diminish.

I am not a fan of a traditional LTC policy because if you never use the policy, the money spent on all of those premiums was wasted. However, for those that are concerned about LTC, we have several other options available, in addition to a traditional LTC policy as described in the following...

Product Riders

There are other was besides LTCI and self-funding that are can help pay for long-term care. And while these are not a replacement for traditional long-term care insurance, there are several insurance carriers nowadays that offer new ways of dealing with the expense of an extended stay in a nursing home.

One way they are retooling to meet people's needs is through optional product riders on life insurance policies. The newest LTC/Life Insurance policies allow you to pay a lump sum or series of premiums to the insurance company in exchange for three benefits in one policy: 1) life insurance benefit should you die; 2) long-term care coverage should you need it, and 3) you can surrender your policy for the available cash value   at any time (subject to possible surrender penalties, and minus the insurance fees you've paid as well as any prior loans or withdrawals taken).

Another policy like the one described above allows you to use your IRA to help fund your LTC protection, which works well when we meet with someone who has a lot of IRA money and not a lot of non-IRA (non-qualified) funds. Those withdrawals will be taxable as income, and may also incur a 10% federal penalty if you withdraw them before age fifty-nine-and-one-half.

Many people prefer to add a product rider to their life insurance policy because they tend to pay less money in premiums. If you are someone who ends up never needing long-term care and you have a policy like this, you haven't thrown all of your money into the void of LTCI. Your policy still remains intact, allowing your family to inherit the available death benefit that the policy provides.

It's important to keep in mind, though, that life insurance with a LTC product rider also has some downsides. It's not a good idea to withdraw the money early, before the age59 ½, or a tax penalty could result. You may also still have to pay taxes on withdrawals. In addition, the amount you can withdraw from your life insurance policy for LTC may not be enough to cover the full costs of a long term care stay. Any withdrawals from the policy for any reason will reduce the policy's available death benefit and cash values, too.

Something else to keep in mind is that you must research your products thoroughly before entering into any kind of policy. Trusting a company to handle your money with care can create risk, so it's important to select carriers that are reputable, who will keep their promises.

I know that it's uncomfortable and possibly irritating to read about long-term care. But that's exactly the reason I want to discuss it: it's easy to gloss over something you aren't interested in. But always remember that when you need long-term care, you're either going to thank or curse your past self for the decisions you made about it. I hope you decide to live without regret!

Spousal Planning

Something to remember when planning for retirement is that you're probably planning for more than one person. Even if you don't think you'll have to deal with expensive healthcare or even long-term care, what about your spouse? When we consider two people rather than one, the odds of one of you dealing with these expenses increase. So when you begin considering potential retirement plans, keep both of you in mind.

It's very important that we plan for making sure that the surviving spouse will help feel secure about retirement after the first spouse dies. Statistically, the husband typically passes away before the wife... some say it's because men want to die first! Haha. Just kidding.[115]

It's very important that you have a plan in place to help protect your loved ones and have a planner that has your best interests in mind.

---

[115] Erin Duffin. Statista. Sept. 30, 2022. "Life expectancy in North America 2020." https://www.statista.com/statistics/274513/life-expectancy-in-north-america/

CHAPTER THIRTY-SEVEN

Retirement Income

W hat does retiring mean for you? Close your eyes and really think about it. What do you imagine yourself doing during your golden years? Perhaps you want to see the world with your spouse, family, or friends. Some are more concerned with staying at home and picking up neglected hobbies like tinkering or gardening.

To do any of the above and more, you must have income. If you don't have enough money to follow through on your goals, you won't be able to sustain your ideal lifestyle, even if it's fairly inexpensive to maintain. I once heard someone compare your income to a blood flow: just like blood keeps the body going, income keeps your lifestyle going. This is exactly why having income is so important to any phase of life, including retirement.

The idea of income can be overwhelming for many people because they don't know where to start. Some think they need to put their entire life savings into one product that they believe will provide them everything they need. That's probably a little too drastic, in my opinion. I always opt for balance over the rumored "easy way out." As you can probably already tell, retirement planning isn't easy, and if it is, there's probably something going wrong somewhere. No one has ever come across the perfect product that works for everyone, and in a way, that's a good thing. You won't ever have the opportunity to settle for one option. With proper planning, you can have a personalized retirement plan that fits your specific needs.

You can do this, believe it or not! A qualified financial professional can guide you through the confusing maze of retirement planning. With a financial professional, you won't just have someone who can help you outline your future, you also will have someone on your side as you make the retirement journey.

Sources of Income

Things can get really intimidating when you start thinking about the puzzle of retirement income. So let's start by laying everything out and then reorganizing them, figuring out ways that portions of income can help you reach your retirement goals.

Social Security

You've probably seen on your pay stubs that a portion of each paycheck goes into Social Security. This source of income plays quite a large role in many retirees' retirement plans. Although Social Security is only meant to supplement other income you might have, it still offers a good amount of money and it's important to take advantage of this program.

Pension

You might be lucky enough to have a pension plan with your employer. If you have one, this is a wonderful and often reliable source of income that you should take full advantage of. If you don't have one, you can skip this section.

Although a pension is a pretty reliable source of income, it's pretty common knowledge at this point that the government and other employers have often neglected their employees' pension funds, which sometimes makes it underfunded. Currently, state pension plans are estimated to be underfunded by $1.4 trillion![116]

You might also want to see what collection offers your pension has. Some pensions offer things like funding your spouse if you are the first to pass away.

Often, a pension plan offers you a lump sum at the beginning of retirement. This helps reduce the company's liabilities, but it might not be the right choice for you. It's always a good idea to discuss your pension options with a financial professional before making any big decisions.

Also, you can search for lost financial accounts by going to your state's website. In Florida you can go to https://www.fltreasurehunt.org and see if you have any unclaimed accounts. Additionally, if you used to live in another state, don't forget to check that state's unclaimed property websites.

Here are some states where many of my Florida retired clients move from:

-**New York**: www.ny.gov/services/find-lost-money
-**New Jersey**: www.unclaimedproperty.nj.gov
-**Connecticut**: www.ctbiglist.com
-**Illinois**: icash.illinoistreasurer.gov
-**California**: ucpi.sco.ca.gov/UCP/Default.aspx
-**Rhode Island**: treasury.ri.gov/treasury-divisions/unclaimed-property

401(k) and IRA

Nowadays, as pension plans continue to dwinde, a popular option for stowing away retirement funds is to have a 401(k), IRA, or equivalent. Although these accounts

---

[116] Equable. Sept. 14, 2022. "Unfunded Liabilities for State Pension Plans in 2022." https://equable.org/unfunded-liabilities-for-state-pension-plans-2022/

are not as good of a deal as pensions, it's usually a good idea to consider using them if they are available.[117]

You might have changed jobs a few times in your life, and in that case, it's important to rediscover any old retirement accounts you may have opened a decade ago. Once you have all your retirement accounts together, you can truly assess how much retirement income you have stowed away.

Other Assets

There are other accounts or policies you might have somewhere or another that can contribute to your overall retirement income. Other sources of income include:

- Life insurance cash values
- Annuities
- Passive income such as rental properties
- Stocks and bonds
- Liquid assets
- Alternative investments

Why am I asking you to bring up all these different sources of income? Because when you're sitting down with your financial professional, it's important to show him or her everything you've got going for you. You might have a couple thousand dollars in an ancient IRA or a small share in a local grocery store, but everything counts no matter its value.

We meet with people all the time and when we add up all their assets, they are often surprised to discover the value of their net worth today. Many of my clients are quite

---

[117] Nathaniel Lee. CNBC. March 24, 2021. "How 401(k) accounts killed pensions to become one of the most popular retirement plans for U.S. workers." https://www.cnbc.com/2021/03/24/how-401k-brought-about-the-death-of-pensions.html

conservative in their spending. Oftentimes their parents went through The Great Depression, so they learned from a young age to save not spend and live below their means. As such, they have built up a nice retirement portolio and they're looking for the best strategies to have that retirement portfolio take care of them for the rest of their lives.

Retirement Income Needs

Many people have a difficult time figuring out just how much income they will need during retirement. Some might have a decent idea of what they need, but others come to shockingly random numbers that hinder more than help their retirement plan. Many think that all they need is a million dollars to keep up their lifestyle. It's quite possible that saving this much money will get you through retirement, but I think it's too risky nonetheless, and it probably won't serve you to its full potential to simply have a dollar amount saved for retirement.

I don't just hope that my clients have enough to last them; I work with them to increase their chances as much as possible. There are better ways to plan for retirement than wishing yourself luck.

Goals and Dreams

The biggest allure of retirement is the idea that you can renew yourself in a way. Without the demands of work, you can finally complete demanding projects and goals. Although we might have a vague idea of what we'd like our retirement to look like, we unfortunately don't want to look at things in detail. It has been my experience that some spend more time planning their next vacation than managing their finances. If this is the case, it might help to consider your retirement as an extended vacation. That way, it won't feel so much like a chore!

When you think about it, you can make your retirement anything you want it to be. For some, the dream is to live abroad in a place like Italy or Spain. For others, their retirement "vacations" would mean volunteering at a homeless shelter or auditing classes at the local university. Some might want to deepen their personal relationships, and others want to revive their interest in an old hobby, like scrapbooking, jewelry-making or photography. There are others that would like to begin a new business by selling their artwork or skills (Be careful about starting a small business late in life!)

Retirement is your time. It's the time you should be free to ask yourself what you truly want to do.

Once you've determined this, cost must be considered. What are the costs of, say, a trip to Iceland? What about a road trip around the country? I know a couple who had the dream of taking each grandchild on a trip out-of-country each year. That is a lofty and admirable goal and can create amazing memories with your family.

For many, the biggest joy in life is spending quality time with children and grandchildren. Taking them on vacation or just having the flexibility to visit them is incredibly rewarding. We want our clients to have as many of those "best days" as possible.

Current Budget

A part of retirement planning that trips some people up is the idea of a budget. Many retirees assume that when they retire, that they will be able to cut many expenses. They believe that if they don't have to pay for gas, work clothing, and contributions to savings anymore that they will have overall fewer expenses.

The problem is our spending is often underestimated. When I ask my clients about their spending, they often tell me a number that seems measly. After they tell me this number, I ask them where they got it from, and they tell me they estimate by looking at their bills. The problem is, nobody's overall spending is only made up of things like the mortage and groceries.

Once they tell me about their estimates based on bills, I begin to ask more questions. I ask them how many starbucks coffees they have each month, what they spent during the latest department store sale, and how many people in their life receive birthday gifts. As we continue to discuss spending, my clients begin to see the reality of their total spending.

Besides this everyday spending, retirees sometimes spend a great amount on their children and grandchildren. They want to help pay for their child's or grandchild's college, or help them get by for a month by paying a monthly electricity bill. This isn't something that happens every now and then, either. Some parents I know through our business acknowledge that they give substantial funding to their adult children, sometimes into their late twenties and even thirties. This isn't always a bad thing, because the feeling you get from helping your kids out can be incredibly rewarding. I'm not saying to stop giving your kids money, but I am saying you need to take this spending into account when you're putting together your expense report.

Also keep in mind that sometimes your child might ask you for something large – like helping them with a downpayment on their home. On big decisions such as this, be sure to make a logical decision not an emotional one. You have to make sure that you can afford that gift and that it won't impact your standard of living in the future. Even if your child promises to pay it back, assume the worst that you'll never see that money again and make sure that you'll be financially okay long-term with that decision.

Also, let's say you're giving $50,000 to help a child buy a house, it's very important for you to work with an attorney so that your child and their spouse, if applicable, will both sign a note that they owe you that $50,000 back. This way in case of divorce you'll be paid back the $50,000 plus interest.

Other Expenses

Now that you have your true expense report as well as a list of goals to accomplish in retirement, there are a few more things to consider before your plan is complete. I know you're a motivated person, so let's look into these final aspects of your retirement plan.

Housing

Ask yourself where and how you want to live during retirement.

Many people have invested a lot of work and money into maintaining the house they have, so they want to stay in it for as long as possible. Others would like to move as soon as they reach retirement. Whether you wish to stay or leave your current house, let's consider a few things before making a final decision.

Many of our clients are snowbirds who live up North during the summer and "fly South" for the winter.

Many of my clients want to simplify their lives in retirement. For example, my dad in 2017 sold his 6,000 square foot home in Parkland, Florida, as he doesn't need so much space now that his five kids are all out of the house. He spends the summer at his home in Asheville, North Carolina (a great place to visit, by the way!), but for winters he downsized to a two-bedroom condominium in east Boca Raton on the intercoastal with a view of the ocean. That's ideal retirement snowbird living!

Mortgage

Do you still have a mortgage? Many of my clients are debt-free at this point in their lives, but this might be applicable to you. Having a mortgage during your working years might have helped you tax-wise, but if you're bringing that mortgage with you into retirement things might hurt a bit. Now that you're retired and have limited income, your mortgage isn't doing you any favors. All it's doing is causing you to spend more. It's now imperative that you decide how you want your living space to serve you, whether it be your current home, another home, living abroad, or finding a welcoming retirement or 55+ community.

Upkeep and Taxes

If you have paid off your mortgage, you will still have to pay some form of tax. Although it's easy to brush off annual expenses like taxes as a necessary evil, now that you have a more limited earning potential you might have to pay more in taxes than you expected.

Homeownership doesn't just cost money, but it can also cost you time and energy. As you get older and the kids leave, you'll begin to notice that you're cleaning parts of the house that haven't been lived in for months. You'll find you don't play in the yard with the kids anymore, yet you still mow it every week. Some people are okay with keeping up their house, but others realize that the work doesn't seem worth it in the end.

I once knew a lady who after she had knee surgery that she couldn't even access certain parts of her house. She then hired a housekeeper, but soon felt foolish for having someone clean the entire house even though she only spent her time in about 40% of it.

Practicality and Adaptability

Eric and Elaine wanted to retire in about twenty years or so and had recently sold their home. With busy lives and kids in high school, the couple also had the goal of getting a bigger, better house. After purchasing a large three-story house with a huge kitchen, five bedrooms, and a library, they suddenly realized that when their children moved out, the house would be too large for their twilight years. Much of the house is only accessible by staircase, and the couple were worried about whether or not they will be able to climb those staircases at an older age.

There are other housing situations that might cause problems. I remember a couple who worked for over two years on refurbishing their bathroom, but after the husband had a health scare, their tub and shower were considered safety hazards. As you age it's important to live in a place that looks after you, rather than a place that causes anxiety.

Contracts and Regulations

If you want to move to a completely different state or even a new country, keep the location's new tax table and laws in mind. It's better to inform yourself of it sooner rather than later. That way, you won't be surprised if your expenses increase.

This rule also applies to if you're moving into a retirement community. Read your contract over carefully, several times, before signing. Ask questions about possible scenarios, like if you have to move away before the contract is up. What sorts of penalties, fees, and responsibilities might you have in that situation?

Again, many of my clients are snowbirds but at a certain point they don't want to live that lifestyle anymore as it could be quite expensive and so they no longer want to maintain two homes. Additionally, the maximum deduction for state and local income taxes, sales taxes and property taxes is only $10,000 per year.[118] This might affect homeowners who live in high-tax states such as New York, New Jersey, Connecticut, and California, among others. Please check with your tax professional to see how this might affect you.

Inflation

After low inflation rates for the past decade or two, since the end of the year 2021, the inflation rate has gotten higher.

But the problem doesn't lie in the rate. Although it's been historically low, the buildup over time can be much more expensive than anticipated. You might have bought a home for $50,000 in the seventies, and now a house of the same quality costs something more like $350,000. The truth is, if you retired a few decades earlier, you might have had an easier time funding your lifestyle. This will be true in the next few decades, too. That being said, I recommend that you begin to account for this inevitable inflation in your current retirement plan.

You might be able to cut out some expenses during retirement. A big cost that people might have in retirement would be owning two cars. With ride-share services available such as Uber and Lyft, perhaps you only need one car during retirement which could save you a nice amount of money. Also, relook at your cable bill, home phone and cell phone plans and see if you might be able to save money there as well. Do you even need a home phone nowadays?

Aging

---

[118] IRS.gov. Mar. 3, 2023. "Topic No. 503 Deductible Taxes." https://www.irs.gov/taxtopics/tc503

Retirement is the time you want to relax as you age. We all know we will age eventually, so I recommend that you look at things realistically. Unfortunately, because we all age, things will happen to us. You can choose whether you want to be prepared for that or not. It's hard to think about, but it's absolutely necessary.

Like I discussed a few chapters back, it is very possible that you could spend some time in a long-term care facility of some kind. It's nice to think that we won't be a part of the roughly 70% of Americans that will need it, but planning doesn't only consider the good situations; planning considers the worst situations while hoping of the best.

If this kind of talk still makes you uncomfortable, I suggest you find a way to voice it. Like any skill, talking about long-term care, aging, and the inevitable end takes practice. Surround yourself with people who will listen and not judge you. And don't judge yourself.

I've already discussed the high expense of long-term care in this book, so just remember: Although it's a painful discussion topic for most people, often it's something you have no control over when faced with it. You'll either need nursing home care or you won't, so plan for both.

If you are one of the lucky ones who will never have to live in a nursing home, you should still plan ahead, for every situation. Many retirees underestimate how long they will live... The problem is, what if you assume you'll live to age ninety but you make it to one hundred? Will you have enough funds to cover yet another decade of life?

Assembling the Retirement Plan Puzzle

Now that you have all your planning factors like aging and inflation, how do you feel? Going over all your expenses may make you feel like throwing in the towel, but I know that considering every aspect of your retirement plan can offer significant benefits throughout retirement. You and your financial planner can now work together to put together a plan designed to greatly benefit you in the long-term.

You've probably noticed that all your expenses are unique to you. You spend money on a special assortment of things to fulfill your personal needs and interests. The same will go for your retirement plan: Everything about this plan centers around the goal of fulfilling you and your dreams. Figuring out this plan isn't easy, and there's no one product out there that will suit you and you alone. You will work with your financial professional to decide how to diversify your portfolio.

You might be wondering just how this plan might work and how a financial professional can help you. I'll give you one example: your advisor can help you lower your taxes. Yes, you heard me right!

You've probably heard about the many different retirement accounts you can have, like a 401(k) or an IRA. Some of these retirement accounts will make you pay taxes when you withdraw money from them, but with the help of your advisor, you can discover ways that allow you to take distributions without moving you into a higher tax bracket. This tax planning technique doesn't necessarily expand your income but it helps you keep what you already have saved.

We use a planning software in our firm called Holistiplan to help our clients do tax planning in conjunction with their accountant. Holistiplan shows us what tax bracket you're in now and exactly how much we can do with our S.R.I. Strategic Roth Integration plan to take advantage of today's tax rates before they are scheduled to go up in 2026.

A financial professional can also help you fill in any gaps in your retirement plan. Depending on your needs and goals, you might need an additional source of income or a new preservation method. A financial advisor can guide you toward policies and products that help you fulfill your needs.

Again, I know all this planning might make your head spin. But remember that once you're finished working, you no longer make your paycheck. All your income will be withdrawn from your life's savings, and the best way to do that is to have a personal retirement plan that meets your specific needs.

CHAPTER THIRTY-EIGHT

Annuities

As a financial advisor, I am able to recommend many different types of investment products to my clients. As an insurance agent, I can also offer many individual products and insurance companies that offer their own variation of those products. There are so many, in fact, that just thinking about the number is exhausting. But in this chapter, I want to discuss one product in particular: annuities.

Although I've often reiterated that there is no magic product available that can fix everyone's financial woes, I still meet with people who believe it, even after I explain this to them. Like turning straw into gold, a tale told in the fairytale, Rumpelstiltskin, some people assume advisors can wave a magic financial wand to change years' worth of savings into a strategy for retirement income.

Yet, finances aren't magic; it takes lots of hard work and, typically, several financial products and strategies to generate a complete retirement plan. The most confusing of all products to my clients tends to be the annuity. They've often heard stories and television commercials that demonize the product, or they make assumptions about the product, thinking it's something that it's not. It's my goal in this chapter to explain all the ins and outs of annuities so you can be more informed about them.

An annuity is a type of a guaranteed insurance contract. At its core, any kind of insurance contract is designed to mitigate risk. Car, home, and life insurance help protect your finances in case of certain situations like an accident, damage, or death.

Remember what we discussed earlier about people having longer lifespand than ever before? Annuities are what can help protect you in case you live a long life. Think about it: living longer causes financial risk! Annuities are there to help you throughout your lifetime. That way, if you live a decade or two longer than planned, you can still have reliable income.

How does this work? Basically, you pay an insurance company a premium or series of premium payments at the time you puruchase the contract. Once you do so, the insurance company offers you the option of having them pay you a series of guaranteed income payments for a certain amount of time. How that company pays you, for how long and how much are determined by the annuity contract you have with the insurance company.

Annuitization

I'm not a big fan of annuitization. Annuitization is one way an annuity provides you income. This is basically the process of switching on your flow of money from the annuity. This is a process that cannot be undone.

If you live longer than assumed by you and the company, you'll continue to get regular income for the rest of your life. But if you pass away before your estimated time, the company may keep the rest of the money you put into the annuity (unless you select a payout feature that allows for your beneficiaries to receive a certain portion of any unpaid benefits). This isn't a good situation if you wanted to pass on that money to your heirs.

At my firm, we like to call this "annuicide" because you lose control of your principal. Our clients don't typically want to lose control of their principal, which is why we typically to not recommend that our clients annuitize.

No annuity is exactly the same, and many are newer models with new traits. There may be one out there that fits your goals and needs.

Riders

Above I mentioned that there are many new types of annuities available today that offer you different options and more control over your principal. One of the ways annuities offer you these options is through riders. You will often be charged an annual fee for a rider, which is generally optional. Depending on who you are and your situation, you might want to consider these different riders. Discuss these with your financial advisor; he or she can probably refer you to different products that offer riders:

- Lifetime income rider: Allows for potentially increased or more flexible lifetime income
- Death benefit rider: Allows your beneficiaries to receive a specified amount after you pass away
- Return of premium rider: Allows you or your beneficiaries to claim the original premium paid
- Long-term care rider: Allows an amount of your annuity to pay for long term care should you require it

This isn't an extensive look, and usually the riders have fancier names based on the issuing company, but those are the basics.

Types of Annuities

Although things vary from product to product, there are four basic annuity types: immediate, variable, fixed, and fixed index.

Immediate

Immediate annuities are probably the kind you've heard warnings about before. In my experience, not many people opt for this type of annuity anymore. When you take out an immediate annuity, you are often required to annuitize immediately. First you pay a premium, and then you begin receiving income from it. As we discussed above, once annuitization takes place, you can't go back and you lose control of your principal which my clients don't want to do.

Variable

We don't use variable annuities in our firm as I discussed in my Kiplinger article which can also be found in this book. People often ask me, they say Craig, why don't you like variable annuities? And I say that variable annuities often have more risk than my retired clients like, and the complex fees in a variable annuity can be quite high. So higher risk and higher fees are typically not what my clients are looking for.

A variable annuity relies on underlying mutual fund investments to work properly. When you open up a variable annuity, you pay a premium to the company and they pool your money with other annuity owners and invest in mutual funds. Because the money is invested in the market, it's important to remember that your money is subject to market fluctuations. Another factor to consider with a variable annuity is the potential for higher fees.

You'll probably have to pay more in terms of investment and management fees.

Many variable annuities have relatively higher fees because they are both an insurance product and an investment product. I have seen in my practice variable annuity fees totaling as high as 4% and 5% per year! That's 4% to 5% off the top before you make a dime.

If you died while owning a variable annuity, your family should collect a death benefit. However most people don't buy variable annuities for its life insurance benefit when they die, they buy them to live on because annuities are typically income products. And between the combination of high fees and market risk we don't feel they are suitable investments for retirees. We do not sell variable annuities in my practice as they are generally not appropriate for someone looking to preserve their principal.

 To learn why we don't think variable annuities are suitable investments for many retirees, watch our video on ourwebsite at KirsnerWealth.com.

Fixed

This kind of annuity is pretty simple. You purchase a contract with a guaranteed interest rate and earn that interest rate for the time period specifed in the contract. It's called a MYGA, or a Multi-Year Guaranteed Annuity. For example, if you buy a five-year MYGA, the insurance company pays you a fixed interest rate for those five years. You usually can take out the interest you earn each year or let it grow at the insurance company if you don't need it for income. However, you typically can't touch your principal for those five years without a penalty (surrender charge) that varies by insurance company.

The good news is that your principal is guaranteed by the insurance company and you can calculate the value of your fixed annuity over the interest rate period of your contract exactly. When the interest rate period is up, you can cancel the annuity or restart a new guaranteed interest rate period at current interest rates.

Fixed Index Annuity

Take another look at all the different types of annuities I mentioned so far. Variable annuities relied on the stock market in order to create growth for you. Fixed annuities grow at a fixed rate with principal protection and generally help preserve your savings better than variable annuities.

Now let's consider the fixed index annuity. With a fixed index annuity, you are able to earn interest that is tied to the performance of an external index such as the S&P 500 without ever being invested in the market. They also help protect from market downturns, helping to keep your principal protected.

Instead of your principal growing a specified rate, it has the potential to receive interest credits each year based on the positive growth of a separate market index like the S&P 500. You don't invest in the S&P 500 directly, but the insurance company will credit your annuity interest based on the S&P 500's gains. For example, an annuity contract based on the S&P 500's growth, with a cap rate of 10%, for example, means that if the S&P 500 goes up 10% or more over the next year, you earn 10%. If the S&P 500 goes up 7%, you earn 7%. They most important part is that the insurance company locks in your interest earnings every year. You can never lose those locked-in earnings. For example, in this case in a year that the S&P 500 gains 11%, your annuity value would increase 10%.

These guaranteed products were never designed to beat the market.

The most important part for a retiree especially, is that with a fixed index annuity since your money isn't invested in the market, if the market nosedives (2000, 2008 and 2022, anyone?), you won't see any increase in your contract value. Conversely, there will also be no decrease in your contract value due to the market loss (although any optional rider fees will continue to be assessed each year).

If you would rather have protected principal more than substantial growth potential, it's possible that a fixed index annuity will work for you.

People like the idea of a portion of their money potentially going up when the S&P 500 goes up, but never losing that money when the markets go down. They provide guarantees that are backed by large, established, highly-rated insurance companies, with competitive growth potential.

Other Things to Know About Annuities

As you read above, there are several different kinds of annuities you can choose from. Although a variable annuity might seem very different from an immediate annuity, each have things in common. All annuities, like any other financial vehicle, involves fees and expenses. You need to understand each products' terms, conditions, and restrictions, too.

When considering any annuity, their guarantees are only as sturdy as the company that offers them. Keep this in mind as you research the companies you're considering opening an annuity with. Always ask your financial advisor about his or her opinions on certain companies and products.

Annuities are tax-deferred, meaning you don't have to pay taxes upfront and on interest earnings as the contract value grows. Instead, you will pay ordinary income taxes on your withdrawals. These are meant to be long-term products, so, like other tax-deferred or tax-advantaged products, if you begin taking withdrawals from your contract before age fifty-nine-and-one-half, you may have to pay a 10% federal tax penalty. Also, while annuities are generally considered illiquid, most contracts allow you to withdraw up to 10% of your contract value every year without a penalty. More than that and you could incur penalties.

When people retire, for those that have lost money in the markets in the past, they like the idea of protected money that is tied to the growth of the S&P 500 but not actually at risk when the S&P 500 goes down.

Not everyone wants or needs an annuity in their retirement plan, but you should at least consider them. Having annuities and their various types in mind is just one way of being informed of your options. Whether or not annuities seem appealing to you at this time, I'd recommend talking to your advisor about them and getting their opinion. They will be able to better explain each individual product in detail. They'll help evaluate your goals and find a product that might help you achieve them.

CHAPTER THIRTY-NINE

How to Save Money on Your Life Insurance

Most of my clients are retired and have won the game of wealth. As such, they generally don't need life insurance. However, many of my clients do have older life insurance policies that often can be improved with a modern, more efficient life insurance policy for several reasons...

For example, let's say you're seventy years old, have an old whole life policy from 1992 with a $100,000 death benefit and $60,000 of cash value in the policy. Here are some facts you should know about this policy:

1) <u>Your internal cost of insurance on this policy is high</u>!

That old life insurance policy uses the 1990 census mortality table, which calculates its internal costs on how long people were living back in 1990. That old census table is what the insurance company uses to calculate how much it charges you for your cost of insurance each year. The fact is people are living much longer now, so a modern policy might charge you lower costs than an old policy, even if you are older now than when you first took out the policy, as long as you qualify health-wise.

2) <u>Having high cash value within your life insurance policy often doesn't do your family any good</u>!

For example, if you have a life insurance policy with a $100,000 death benefit and $60,000 of cash value, you really only have $40,000 of actual life insurance because when you die the insurance company keeps the $60,000 cash value and only gives your family $100,000!

A modern policy might give you as much as double the life insurance benefit, $200,000, of life insurance using that same $60,000 of cash value! That's a lot of leverage. And we can do what's called a 1035 tax free exchange and move your $60,000 of cash value directly from your old, inefficient life insurance policy to the new, efficient life insurance policy without paying any income taxes! So, you're moving money from one pocket to the other and getting significantly more life insurance death benefit from a large, highly-rated company. Keep in mind, though, that often times older policies have richer guarantees and benefits than newer policies available, so you'll want to do a careful analysis of both the old and new policy to weigh all benefits, costs, guarantees, and more.

One potential downside typically is that you can't cash in that new policy for all its cash value right away, especially since you'll have a new surrender penalty period. If you did decide to cash in the policy you would be forced to pay ordinary income tax gains on all the accrued interest within the policy, which could be a substantial amount of taxable gains.

Our clients typically aren't interested in the cash value. They want the most death benefit for the least amount of money!

3) <u>Modern life insurance policies can include long-term care benefits</u>!

As I discussed in the long-term care section of this book, modern life insurance policies from large, highly-rated insurance companies might include a rider that allows you to use your $200,000 death benefit, for example, while you're alive to help pay for long-term care costs. For example, we might set up this policy so you can use up to $4,000 per month or $48,000 per year for four years if you need long-term care support.

This could be a significant improvement on an old policy. Of course, we must do a complete comparison of the old policy versus the new to make sure the switch makes sense for you. Obviously, never cancel your old life insurance policy until you have a formal approved offer for the new life insurance policy and that new policy is in force with a check paid to the new insurance company.

4) <u>What is life expectancy pricing</u>?

Many average life insurance agents sell life insurance policies with level premiums to age 120 or age 100 when not many people actually live that long! Why overpay for your life insurance policy? The less you pay in premiums, the better return on investment your family could potentially receive when you die. So, when it makes sense for our clients, we use what we call life expectancy pricing and what that means is we design the policy so that you pay the lowest level premium to age 95, or whatever age you're comfortable with. Paying level premiums to age 95 versus level premiums to age

120 could save you as much as 20% each year in premiums!

Now you might be wondering, what if I'm alive at age 96? Well, the good news is that you can keep this policy in force to your age 120 if you live that long! The premiums will be substantially higher at age 96. However, you may have saved so much money through age 95 that from a time value of money standpoint, you're still ahead!

5) <u>We shop the life insurance marketplace for you.</u>

Some insurance agents are "captive agents," which means they must do business with their main life insurance company first. We are independent and work with many of the largest and highest-rated insurance companies around.

Many agents only shop with one life insurance company when trying to get you a new policy. However, we have you examined one time and shop three to six companies at the same time to get you more options to choose from! If we get one company to give you a "Standard" life insurance rating, we may be able to go to the other insurance company and say to them if you give us a "Preferred" rating, you'll get the deal and they may be able to give us that "Preferred" rating!

6) <u>What is a life settlement</u>?

If you have a life insurance policy that is more than two years old which you no longer need or want any more, a life settlement allows you to sell your old life insurance policy for potentially far more than you could get if you cashed that policy in for its cash surrender value. Now, this only works if you are over age seventy-five, unless your health has gotten significantly worse than when you first took out the policy (and in that case, you might want to keep the policy for your family's benefit!).

For example, let's say you are a seventy-eight-year-old male with an old $500,000 life insurance policy that you're paying $10,000 per year in premiums, it has a cash surrender value of $50,000, and you no longer want the policy. You might be able to get you a life settlement payout on this policy of $75,000, which is $25,000 more than you would have gotten if you had cashed it in, and you don't have to pay the $10,000 in premiums any longer, which saves you money!

Who buys life settlements? Large banks and hedge funds often buy these policies. Then they put your policy in a blind pool with other policies, which is serviced by a company that monitors these policies on the bank's behalf. These transactions can be complicated and involve a number of requirements and limitations, so be sure to work with a qualified insurance agent and advisor if you're considering a life settlement.

7) What are the three types of life insurance policies?

a. Whole life. Whole life is typically the most expensive type of life insurance and is designed to build up cash value. Most of my clients only use their life insurance primarily for the death benefit, so this high cash value usually doesn't do them much good. They essentially "overpaid" for their life insurance benefit.

b. Term insurance. Term is generally the least expensive type of life insurance where you are covered for a level premium for a certain period of time. For example, a ten- or thirty-year level term policy with level premiums for the ten or thirty years. This is often useful when you have young children and need more coverage to help protect your family should an untimely death occur earlier on in life.

c. Universal life insurance. This is designed to last your entire life, like whole life, but be less expensive because it's not designed solely to build up significant cash value like a whole life policy does, rather it's designed to offer you more flexibility in how and when you pay premiums (assuming you pay enough to keep the coverage inforce). Where is the cash value? It's in your pocket in "saved premiums." This is the type of insurance we prefer for many of our clients because it tends to provide you the most permanent life insurance for the lowest possible premiums.

Now, you might be wondering why old universal life policies had problems. If you bought a universal life policy in the 1980s or 1990s it was likely based on projected interest rates of perhaps 8% or 9% per year. Well, as you know, interest rates have mostly been going down for the past thirty years so those high projected interest rates didn't last and you were probably forced to pay much more in premiums than you might have expected. My dad always says, instead of "vanishing premiums" the only thing that vanished was the agent!

Modern universal life insurance policies are based on guaranteed interest rates with no moving parts like the old policies had, so you don't have any surprises. Or if they are based on current interest rates, the projected rates are likely lower and more reasonable to assume based on current interest rates. And if interest rates rise in the future (as I believe will happen because everything is cyclical), you might be able to pay a lower premium in the future.

Note: A word of caution against variable life insurance policies. I mentioned earlier in this book I don't often recommend variable annuities, and I also don't often recommend variable life insurance policies because your cash value is at risk due to stock market fluctuations, less the cost of insurance fees.

CHAPTER FORTY

Social Security

For many people, Social Security plays a huge role in their retirement plan.

Your first real paycheck (mine was from working at my dad's financial planning office at age 11), suddenly makes you pay taxes and Social Security. Since the days of the Great Depression, Social Security has been an immensely popular program.

Social Security on the surface is quite simple: if you've paid towards it for ten years or more, you are able to receive benefits during retirement for the rest of your life.

Lots of Americans at this point in time are quite worried that Social Security is dying, which will cause you to miss out on these benefits.

Is Social Security Dying?

It seems as if more and more people are asking this question these days. It often appears as titles of financial articles and people discuss it all the time on the news. People wonder if Social Security is dying because the program is notoriously underfunded, and the increasing number of retirees out there isn't lightening the burden in any way. But the biggest sufferers of this underfunded system, according to many, are the younger generations who might not experience a penny of Social Security benefits.

This question is ever-present as headlines trumpet an underfunded Social Security program, alongside the sea of baby boomers retiring in droves and the comparatively smaller pool of younger people who are funding the system.

The Social Security Administration itself acknowledges this concern as each Social Security statement now contains a link to its website (ssa.gov) and a page entitled, "Will Social Security Be There For Me?"

Just a reminder, as if you needed one, that nothing in life is guaranteed. Additionally, depending on who you're listening to, Social Security funds may run low before 2034 thanks to the financial instability and government spending that accompanied the 2020 COVID-19 pandemic.

Before you get too discouraged, though, here are a few thoughts to keep you going:

- 77 cents to the dollar after 2034 might not sound like a lot is being lopped off your check, but as you can see, at least you're getting more than half of your original benefit.[119]
- Social Security is doing its best to make changes to their system. Most recently they have worked to help protect their funds by raising full retirement age and clearing up loopholes.
- Congress is also doing their part to get things fixed, by implementing full retirement age as well as eligibility.

---

[119] CNBC. October 13, 2022. "Will Social Security run out of money? Here's what could happen to your benefits if Congress doesn't act." https://www.cnbc.com/select/will-social-security-run-out-heres-what-you-need-to-know/

- The Social Security system has fulfilled their promises to those who've retired already, and those soon to retire should have nothing to worry about.

At this point, even people who aren't ready to retire can probably assume they will at least get some amount of Social Security. If you ask the question "Will I receive Social Security?" the answer is yes. It'll be yes until it becomes no.

Lots of us are worried we won't get our share of Social Security because it would put a huge dent in our retirement plan. So many of us are heavily — if not completely — reliant on Social Security. Would you believe me if I told you that, on average, Social Security is worth about 33% of a retiree's income? About half of all couples and over 70% of single people said that their Social Security was worth around 50% of their entire retirement income.[120]

I would have to say, Social Security probably plays a significant role in your retirement plan.

Something else that might concern soon-to-be retirees is that no one is legally allowed to give you advice on your Social Security benefits.

That might sound odd, and you're probably wondering why I'm here talking about it. And you're probably wondering about that one time you discussed your benefits with a Social Security representative on the phone. Didn't he or she give you advice?

It's true that those who work for the Social Security Administration are well-informed and available to help you if you need it. They know the system inside and out and can easily explain how to go through the processes

---

[120] Social Security Administration. 2023. "Fact Sheet: Social Security." https://www.ssa.gov/news/press/factsheets/basicfact-alt.pdf

correctly. The government, however, says that because you are the one who's been contributing and benefiting from Social Security, you are the one responsible for your Social Security decisions.

Financial professionals still have to abide by the same law, BUT, some highly trained professionals have found ways to help. They are able to assist you as you work to implement strategies. These strategies can help you get your maximum benefits from Social Security. Remember that your situation, goals, and needs are all personally yours. When it comes to anything, including Social Security, things need to be catered to you. How can your advisor help you do this?

When it comes to Social Security, you have a few choices to make. First, you could choose to begin taking your benefits on the day you qualify for them (you'll qualify at a certain age, depending on how old you are right now). Taking out benefits earlier means you'll likely be receiving income for longer, but usually those checks will be worth less money. Instead of taking your benefits on the first day, you can choose to wait on those funds until you get older. If you do this, your benefits will be higher. Discussing these important decisions with your financial advisor is a great way to figure out which path you should take.

So even though you need to make your decisions by yourself, it's handy to have someone that knows what they're doing. You can gain a lot of perspective once you hear about all the options you have and it will probably benefit you more in the long run.

Having a financial professional who is willing to help you out even though he or she doesn't get paid to offer that information and guidance, may be a sign you have a quality advisor. I believe that knowledge and passion for their work, plus an obligation to fulfill your needs as a retiree, are among the best traits you can find in an advisor.

Full Retirement Age

Social Security seems too good to be true for some people. All they really care about is that they have it, with no further questions asked. I'd say this practice should be stopped. Once you know about all your options within Social Security, you can apply that knowledge to your withdrawal strategy.

For example, it's pretty well-known that you can begin taking out Social Security at age 62. Because people understand this and it seems like a simple decision, they often take the money without thinking. Some decide to wait on receiving their benefits, but still, the most popular decision is to grab it as soon as possible.[121]

The problem with this decision, however, is all the money you may be leaving behind. How does this work? Well, there are two ways that the Social Security Administration determines the amount of your monthly paycheck. The first is your earnings history and the second is your full retirement age, or FRA. Your earnings history is, put plainly, what kind of money you made throughout your working life. To determine your earnings history, the Social Security Administration takes a look at the 35 years in which you made the most money. They then use a formula to calculate a monthly average for you. Any other years you worked for less are not counted in this formula.

---

[121] Jim Miller. Daily Journal. April 15, 2021. "The most and least popular ages to claim Social Security." https://www.daily-journal.com/life/family/the-most-and-least-popular-ages-to-claim-social-security/article_51ee0af0-9c4f-11eb-8c78-77e20d46b89e.html#:~:text=Age%2062%3A%20This%20is%20the, for%20Social%20Security%20at%2062

After determining your earnings history, the government then looks at your FRA. Based on how close you are to FRA, your check is written for a certain amount.

As you can see in the following chart, the FRA has changed over the years. Like many other factors of the retirement plan, things are changed because of the overall life expectancy in America. What is your FRA?

Age to Receive Full Social Security Benefits*	
(Called "full retirement age" or "normal retirement age.")	
Year of Birth*	FRA
1937 or earlier	65
1938	65 and 2 months
1939	65 and 4 months
1940	65 and 6 months
1941	65 and 8 months
1942	65 and 10 months
1943-1954	66
1955	66 and 2 months
1956	66 and 4 months
1957	66 and 6 months
1958	66 and 8 months
1959	66 and 10 months
1960 and later	67

If you were born on Jan. 1 of any year, you should refer to the previous year. (If you were born on the 1st of the month, we figure your benefit (and your full retirement age) as if your birthday was in the previous month.) [122]

After you reach FRA, you can then receive as much in benefits as you possibly can. 100% of your potential earnings is called the full monthly benefit. For most Baby Boomers to receive their full monthly benefit, they must reach age sixty-six.

Claiming benefits before FRA can cause you to miss out on a lot of potential money. A whopping 5% gets lopped off your monthly paycheck if you decide to take it one year before FRA. If you decide to wait two years before FRA, 10% of the monthly paycheck is taken away. The Social Security Administration will continue to reduce that paycheck by 5% for every year before FRA that you claim benefits. On the other hand, as you pass FRA and continue to wait on benefits, your total earnings increase each waiting year by 8%.

Although there are circumstances when you might want to take out your Social Security early, it's quite possible that the best decision you can make is to wait until age 70 to take out any benefits.

Some of my married retired clients turn on one spouses Social Security early, and the second spouse's they wait to age 70. This way, when one of the spouse's die, the surviving spouse inherits the higher Social Security

---

[122] Social Security. Accessed July 5, 2023. "Starting Your Retirement Benefits Early."
https://www.ssa.gov/benefits/retirement/planner/agereduction.html

payment of the deceased spouse. They also get to enjoy the lower Social Security payment for longer as well.

My Social Security

After age 30, the Social Security Admnistration begins to notify you of your account. This account, called My Social Security, can be set up online and is a great resource that can help you keep track of your benefit options. You will be able to see your earnings so far: everything you have contributed so far throughout your lifetime.

This account is easily activated, and through it you can have a better idea of where you stand in terms of benefits. Many of my clients find the account helpful when they are ready to begin planning for retirement. You can get answers to questions like, "How much money can I expect to get if I take out my money at age sixty-two versus age seventy?" or "How will my spouse benefit from Social Security if I die before him or her?"

This account can also be helpful for spotting issues with your earnings. One woman I know was incredibly diligent when keeping track of her finances. She often compared her tax records with the Social Security earnings on her account, and she once discovered that she wasn't receiving her deserved amount of monthly benefits. Once she notified the Social Security Administration, she received everything they owed her. This is a lesson in being proactive with your finances instead of expecting others to do things for you!

COLA

As you've already read, it's very likely that Social Security will stay around for a while. At this point in time you can count on them to send you the correct amount on monthly benefit no matter what. There is one catch, though, called COLA, or cost-of-living adjustment. This is an adjustment in your Social Security payments. It's the only thing that might affect your earnings, and it's something you have no control over.

The COLA is the Social Security Administration's way of helping you out as inflation occurs. COLA is simply an increase to your benefit as the inflation rate goes up. Consider this similar to a raise when you were working.

In 2022, COLA increased by 8.7% due to rising inflation.[123] However, this rate changes depending on the inflation rate that year. The years 2009, 2010 and 2015 did not have enough inflation to merit a cost-of-living adjustment.

Many people consider COLA to be simply an increase in pay, but I don't think it works that way. Your benefit is increasing, but so is everything else, like gas and groceries. You'll likely be paying more for those things, rather than having money leftover.

Although COLA isn't meant to make you richer than you were before, it is still a blessing to have it nonetheless.

Spousal Benefits

Don't get to thinking that deciding when to take out your Social Security is the only decision you have to make! You also need to make some choices about spousal benefits.

Remember how Social Security calculates your benefit amount based on the 35 years in which you made the most money? Well, many spouses haven't been working for 35 years. Perhaps your spouse has been staying at home and

---

[123] Social Security Administration. "Latest Cost of Living Adjustment." https://www.ssa.gov/oact/cola/latestCOLA.html#:~:text=The%20la test%20COLA%20is%208.7,are%20payable%20in%20January%202 023.

taking care of the kids. Maybe you were the spouse that didn't make nearly as much money as the other. If this is the case, filing for spousal benefits rather than your own benefits might bring about better monetary results.

In order to file for this spousal benefit you must reach age 62 and your spouse (who is assumed to be the breadwinner in your family) should have already filed for their benefits.

Remember, though, that there may be penalties (losing up to as much as 67.5% of the entire check) if you file early at age 62. Also, your check will not go up in value if you delay taking benefits.

With all these things to consider, it's best to go over your own personal money situation before making a decision on taking spousal benefits or not. Perhaps you'll get a better benefit if you choose to take your own Social Security rather than taking the spousal benefits. For others, they'd be better off doing things the opposite way.

Allow me to help you visualize this situation better with a story of a fictional couple, Matthew and Suzy. Matthew is 62 and has been the primary breadwinner in the family, which allows him to take more out in Social Security. Suzy is 60.

If Matthew's FRA is age 66 and he waits until that age to file for benefits, he would be able to qualify for $1,600 worth of benefits per month. If he decides to take the money early at age 62, he would receive $1,200 per month. Suzy would like to take out spousal benefits as early as possible, so she would only have to wait two years to receive them. The problem is, if she took spousal benefits early, she would have to miss out on 67.5% of her potential benefits, leaving her with only $520 a month. As you can probably tell, this is not the best situation the couple could be in. What could they do together to maximize their benefits?

The two of them could wait until FRA, which is age 66. If they do so, Matthew would be able to take out $1,600. Suzy will turn age 62 two years later and at that point she can take out $800 a month in spousal benefits. Overall, the couple's total in benefits per month would increase to $2,400. This is a major difference from the $1,720 they would receive if they didn't wait another six years.

That still isn't the best they could do, though. The couple could wait even longer, until age 70. This is the age that will yield the highest benefit for the couple. If he filed at age 70, Matthew would receive $2,112 a month. Because Suzy's spousal benefits wouldn't increase, she could apply for her benefits at the same time as Matthew. Just the same as she would at age 66, she would receive $800 per month. This combined with Matthew's benefit would raise their overall monthly earnings to $2,912. Compare that with the $1,720 we read about at the beginning! Could you wait a few more years to almost double your Social Security?[124]

All of these calculations are probably quite overwhelming to read. We started with discussing your full retirement age, cost-of-living adjustments, and spousal benefits.

Divorced Spouses

Even for divorced spouses, you still might be able to qualify for spousal benefits. First, though, you must consider a few things. Were you married for over ten years? Have you been divorced for at least two years? Have you stayed unmarried since your divorce? Does your ex-spouse qualify for Social Security? If you answered yes to

---

[124] Social Security Administration. 2023. "Retirement Planner: Benefits For You As A Spouse."
https://www.ssa.gov/oact/quickcalc/spouse.html

all four of these questions, then you'll still be able to qualify for a spousal benefit from your ex-spouse. There is one big difference from applying for benefits when you're divorced: you can apply for your spousal benefit before your ex-spouse applies for his or her benefits.[125]

Let's think about how this would work with another example. Take a couple, Ron and Penny. They had been married for twenty years before they divorced. At this point, Ron was 48 and Penny was 45. Penny didn't remarry but Ron has been remarried for twenty years. Penny hasn't worked for quite a while because she had to take care of her sick mother for several years. This has affected her earnings history quite a lot.

Ron has decided to maximize his Social Security by waiting unttil age 70 to withdraw his benefits. However, after reaching FRA, Penny is ready to receive hers. Even though Ron still hasn't filed for benefits, Penny can still receive hers at anytime she wants.

Widowed Spouses

If your spouse has passed away, you are able to receive a survivor's benefit. This is similar to a spousal or divorce benefit, except that you are able to qualify for your deceased spouse's full benefit, rather than a fraction of it. Another perk you get from this situation is that you can begin taking these benefits as early as age 60. Keep in mind, though, that taking money early, even as a survivor's benefit, will reduce your monthly check.

If your spouse was already taking out Social Security at the time of his or her death, the Social Security Administration allows you to continue taking out that

---

[125] Social Security Administration. 2023. "Retirement Planner: If You Are Divorced."
https://www.ssa.gov/planners/retire/divspouse.html

same amount. You are not allowed to wait until a later age to maximize benefits. The rule is that the widow of a deceased person cannot take out more in benefits than if your spouse would have, if he or she were was still alive.[126]

Taxes

As you have probably noticed throughout this book, just about everything you do in retirement has possible tax repercussions. Even Social Security, believe it or not! It might seem strange that you have to pay taxes, considering you were taxed as you built up the benefits throughout your lifetime. But unfortunately, the government will probably still make you pay taxes when taking benefits out, too. Sometimes you'll have to pay taxes on up to 85% of your benefits.

The Social Security Administration determines how much you are to pay in taxes with something called the provisional income formula. Basically, the formula adds your adjusted gross income, the nontaxable interest (also known as interest from government bonds and notes), and half of your Social Security benefits to determine your provisional income.

After your provisional income is determined, the following chart can show you how much you will pay in Social Security taxes.[127]

---

[126] Social Security Administration. 2023. "Social Security Benefit Amounts For The Surviving Spouse By Year Of Birth." https://www.ssa.gov/planners/survivors/survivorchartred.html

[127] Social Security Administration. 2023. "Benefits Planner: Income Taxes and Your Social Security Benefits." https://www.ssa.gov/benefits/retirement/planner/taxes.html

Taxes on Social Security

Provisional Income = Adjusted Gross Income + Nontaxable Interest + ½ of Social Security

If you are ____ and your provisional income is____, then...		Uncle Sam will tax ___ of your Social Security
Single	Married, filing jointly	
Less than $25,000	Less than $32,000	0%
$25,000 to $34,000	$32,000 to $44,000	Up to 50%
More than $34,000	More than $44,000	Up to 85%

https://www.ssa.gov/planners/taxes.html

This is yet another situation when you'll probably want to consult a financial advisor. With someone to help you out, you'll be able to better calculate how much you need to pay. You'll also get advice from your advisors that will help you develop tax-saving strategies on things like your Social Security benefit.

The Earnings Test

There is one more situation you might find yourself in that may complicate your Social Security benefits.

You may still be under FRA and still working. However, you may be taking out benefits anyway. This might make things a bit difficult.

Because you haven't reached FRA, your benefits are going to be lower than if you had waited. And since you're still working, the Social Security Administration is required to withhold an amount from your check so they can add to your benefits. If you haven't reached FRA, but you started your Social Security benefits and are still working, things get a little hairy.

In order to keep this situation under control, Uncle Sam will administer an "earnings test." As of 2023, if you are under FRA, you are able to make up to $21,240 per year before your Social Security check is reduced. If you are making more than that amount, the Social Security Administration will withhold one dollar for every two dollars you make. When you hit the year you become FRA and you're still working, you can make up to $56,520 per year without your Social Security being docked. But if you make more than that amount, the organization will withhold one dollar for every three dollars you make over.

After you make it to FRA, you no longer have to worry about the earnings test. After that, any money that the Social Security Administration has withheld from you so far will be included on your benefit checks after you reach FRA.[128]

We can help our clients look at their Social Security options to help them understand their options available to them and help determine what might be the best option. Things we look at include: longevity — how long did your parents live? How is your health? Do you have other pensions that we need to look at in relation to this decision? Do you need Social Security now to pay your bills or is it better to wait and get a higher amount later? All of these get factored in to this component of a complete financial plan.

To learn more, call us at 1-800-807-5558 to attend one of our upcoming dinner seminars. We hold them at Ruth's

---

[128] Social Security Administration. 2023. "Exempt Amounts Under the Earnings Test."
https://www.ssa.gov/oact/cola/rtea.html

Chris in Fort Lauderdale or Abe & Louie's Steakhouse in Boca Raton. You can also visit our website at www.KirsnerWealth.com.

<u>Kirsner Wealth Management</u>
5350 West Hillsboro Blvd, Suite 103
Coconut Creek, Florida 33073
1-800-807-5558

www.KirsnerWealth.com

CHAPTER FORTY-ONE

The Kirsner Wealth Management Team

From left:

Janae Jacobs: **Client Operations Manager**
Daliana Garcia: Administrative Assistant

**Chabelie Marte: Operations Manager and
                     Director of Client Relations**

**Sean Burke, M.S.: Vice President and
                     Investment Adviser Representative**

**Craig Kirsner, MBA: Author, Speaker, President
                    & Investment Adviser Representative**

Brianna Shepard: Director of Client Operations

Alexis Lazo: New Business Administrator

CHAPTER FORTY-TWO

Best and Worst Days of the Stock Market

The following graphics illustrate the best and worst days of the stock market in the last century. You'll notice that many of the best and worst days happened very close together. Take a look for yourself.

(Charts detailing "The 100 Best and Worst Market Days" for the S&P 500 from January 1, 2000 through December 31, 2019 are based on charts provided by W.E. Sherman and Co., LLC, and reprinted with permission.)

The 100 Best and Worst Market Days
S&P 500 Jan. 1, 2000 through Dec. 31, 2019

Summary Statistics	Best 100 Days Net Results		Worst 100 Days Net Results	
	Best 100 Days Net Percent Gain	382.15%	Worst 100 Days Net Percent Loss	-383.72%
	Best-100 Gains in Bear Markets	283.07%	Worst-100 Losses in Bear Markets	**-261.55%**
	Best-100 Gains in Bull Markets	99.08%	Worst-100 Losses in Bull Markets	**-118.86%**
	Bear Market share of all Best-100:	**74.07%**	Bear Market share of all Worst-100:	**68.16%**

Rank	Best 100 Days Ranking			Worst 100 Days Ranking		
	Market Date	Percent Change	Market Type*	Market Date	Percent Change	Market Type*
Top 10	10/13/2008	11.5800%	BEAR	10/15/2008	-9.0350%	BEAR
	10/28/2008	10.7890%	BEAR	12/1/2008	-8.9295%	BEAR
	3/23/2009	7.0758%	BEAR	9/29/2008	-8.8068%	BEAR
	11/13/2008	6.9213%	BEAR	10/9/2008	-7.6167%	BEAR
	11/24/2008	6.4723%	BEAR	11/20/2008	-6.7123%	BEAR
	3/10/2009	6.3663%	BEAR	8/8/2011	-6.6634%	BULL
	11/21/2008	6.3248%	BEAR	11/19/2008	-6.1156%	BEAR
	7/24/2002	5.7327%	BEAR	10/22/2008	-6.1013%	BEAR
	9/30/2008	5.4175%	BEAR	4/14/2000	-5.8278%	BULL
	7/29/2002	5.4078%	BEAR	10/7/2008	-5.7395%	BEAR
11 through 25	12/16/2008	5.1360%	BEAR	1/20/2009	-5.2816%	BEAR
	1/3/2001	5.0099%	BEAR	11/5/2008	-5.2677%	BEAR
	12/26/2018	4.9594%	BULL	11/12/2008	-5.1894%	BEAR
	10/20/2008	4.7685%	BEAR	11/6/2008	-5.0264%	BEAR
	3/16/2000	4.7646%	BULL	9/17/2001	-4.9216%	BEAR
	8/9/2011	4.7487%	BULL	2/10/2009	-4.9121%	BEAR
	10/15/2002	4.7336%	BEAR	8/4/2011	-4.7820%	BULL
	8/11/2011	4.6290%	BULL	9/17/2008	-4.7141%	BEAR
	5/10/2010	4.3974%	BULL	9/15/2008	-4.7136%	BEAR
	4/5/2001	4.3680%	BEAR	3/2/2009	-4.6620%	BEAR
	1/21/2009	4.3491%	BEAR	2/17/2009	-4.5559%	BEAR
	9/18/2008	4.3342%	BEAR	8/18/2011	-4.4594%	BULL
	11/30/2011	4.3315%	BEAR	8/10/2011	-4.4152%	BULL
	10/16/2008	4.2507%	BEAR	3/12/2001	-4.3181%	BEAR
	3/18/2008	4.2410%	BEAR	4/20/2009	-4.2790%	BEAR
26 through 50	11/4/2008	4.0826%	BEAR	3/5/2009	-4.2532%	BEAR
	3/12/2009	4.0729%	BEAR	11/14/2008	-4.1699%	BEAR
	9/19/2008	4.0257%	BEAR	9/3/2002	-4.1536%	BEAR
	2/24/2009	4.0103%	BEAR	2/5/2018	-4.0979%	BULL
	8/14/2002	4.0047%	BEAR	10/2/2008	-4.0291%	BEAR
	10/1/2002	4.0023%	BEAR	8/24/2015	-3.9414%	BULL
	12/2/2008	3.9941%	BEAR	5/20/2010	-3.8976%	BULL
	10/11/2002	3.9059%	BEAR	10/6/2008	-3.8518%	BEAR
	8/26/2015	3.9034%	BULL	7/19/2002	-3.8352%	BEAR
	9/24/2001	3.8983%	BEAR	1/4/2000	-3.8345%	BULL
	12/5/2000	3.8922%	BEAR	9/22/2008	-3.8237%	BEAR
	4/18/2001	3.8890%	BEAR	2/8/2018	-3.7536%	BULL
	12/8/2008	3.8387%	BEAR	11/9/2011	-3.6695%	BEAR
	4/9/2009	3.8053%	BEAR	3/24/2003	-3.5231%	BULL
	5/8/2002	3.7504%	BEAR	3/30/2009	-3.4819%	BEAR
	3/11/2008	3.7130%	BEAR	2/27/2007	-3.4725%	BULL
	7/5/2002	3.6730%	BEAR	2/23/2009	-3.4699%	BEAR
	12/5/2008	3.6499%	BEAR	10/24/2008	-3.4511%	BEAR
	4/1/2008	3.5896%	BEAR	6/4/2010	-3.4411%	BULL
	3/17/2003	3.5427%	BEAR	4/3/2001	-3.4393%	BEAR
	11/26/2008	3.5328%	BEAR	8/5/2002	-3.4296%	BEAR
	10/10/2002	3.4966%	BEAR	9/9/2008	-3.4138%	BEAR
	10/19/2000	3.4743%	BEAR	7/10/2002	-3.3962%	BEAR
	3/13/2003	3.4457%	BEAR	1/14/2009	-3.3460%	BEAR
	1/4/2019	3.4340%	BULL	1/29/2009	-3.3120%	BEAR

The 100 Best and Worst Market Days (cont.)
S&P 500 Jan. 1, 2000 through Dec. 31, 2019

Rank	Best 100 Days Ranking			Worst 100 Days Ranking		
	Market Date	Percent Change	Market Type*	Market Date	Percent Change	Market Type*
	10/27/2011	3.4291%	BEAR	7/22/2002	-3.2911%	BEAR
	8/23/2011	3.4285%	BEAR	10/10/2018	-3.2864%	BULL
	10/10/2011	3.4125%	BEAR	12/4/2018	-3.2365%	BULL
	5/4/2009	3.3868%	BEAR	5/6/2010	-3.2354%	BULL
	1/28/2009	3.3558%	BEAR	9/27/2002	-3.2259%	BEAR
	10/13/2000	3.3381%	BEAR	2/5/2008	-3.1995%	BEAR
	4/25/2000	3.3276%	BULL	9/22/2011	-3.1883%	BEAR
	1/2/2003	3.3200%	BEAR	8/21/2015	-3.1851%	BULL
	4/17/2000	3.3084%	BULL	10/27/2008	-3.1764%	BEAR
	5/27/2010	3.2876%	BULL	12/20/2000	-3.1296%	BEAR
	8/8/2002	3.2722%	BEAR	2/4/2010	-3.1141%	BULL
	5/30/2000	3.2242%	BULL	9/20/2001	-3.1060%	BEAR
	3/17/2009	3.2140%	BEAR	6/29/2010	-3.1017%	BULL
	1/2/2009	3.1608%	BEAR	6/6/2008	-3.0889%	BEAR
	7/7/2010	3.1331%	BULL	10/24/2018	-3.0864%	BULL
	5/18/2009	3.0389%	BULL	10/21/2008	-3.0800%	BEAR
	8/6/2002	2.9919%	BEAR	6/22/2009	-3.0600%	BULL
	12/20/2011	2.9825%	BEAR	2/18/2000	-3.0376%	BULL
	7/15/2009	2.9630%	BULL	9/19/2002	-3.0065%	BEAR
	6/10/2010	2.9507%	BULL	1/7/2009	-3.0010%	BEAR
	9/1/2010	2.9505%	BULL	9/4/2008	-2.9922%	BEAR
	11/28/2011	2.9240%	BEAR	8/5/2019	-2.9778%	BULL
	9/18/2007	2.9208%	BULL	8/9/2007	-2.9650%	BULL
	11/13/2007	2.9093%	BULL	9/1/2015	-2.9576%	BULL
51 through 100	11/7/2008	2.8855%	BEAR	8/1/2002	-2.9574%	BEAR
	4/2/2009	2.8727%	BEAR	9/21/2011	-2.9390%	BEAR
	8/5/2008	2.8719%	BEAR	11/7/2007	-2.9370%	BULL
	6/17/2002	2.8691%	BEAR	6/26/2008	-2.9365%	BEAR
	4/18/2000	2.8663%	BULL	12/4/2008	-2.9308%	BEAR
	9/7/2011	2.8646%	BEAR	8/14/2019	-2.9293%	BULL
	11/28/2007	2.8560%	BULL	1/24/2003	-2.9233%	BEAR
	5/16/2001	2.8453%	BEAR	7/2/2002	-2.9145%	BULL
	8/29/2011	2.8280%	BEAR	1/17/2008	-2.9093%	BEAR
	11/27/2002	2.7986%	BEAR	7/16/2010	-2.8819%	BULL
	3/26/2018	2.7157%	BULL	1/29/2002	-2.8613%	BEAR
	1/7/2000	2.7090%	BULL	12/11/2008	-2.8524%	BEAR
	4/10/2001	2.7066%	BEAR	10/3/2011	-2.8451%	BEAR
	2/6/2009	2.6896%	BEAR	8/11/2010	-2.8179%	BULL
	5/26/2009	2.6302%	BULL	10/30/2009	-2.8065%	BULL
	4/2/2003	2.6116%	BULL	1/2/2001	-2.8032%	BEAR
	6/2/2010	2.5843%	BULL	11/1/2011	-2.7942%	BEAR
	12/3/2008	2.5836%	BEAR	1/24/2000	-2.7634%	BULL
	6/1/2009	2.5818%	BULL	1/28/2000	-2.7457%	BULL
	10/30/2008	2.5804%	BEAR	10/9/2002	-2.7287%	BEAR
	3/9/2000	2.5602%	BULL	12/24/2018	-2.7112%	BULL
	3/27/2001	2.5575%	BEAR	2/29/2008	-2.7090%	BEAR
	3/21/2000	2.5566%	BULL	7/18/2002	-2.7019%	BEAR
	1/2/2013	2.5403%	BULL	7/23/2002	-2.7017%	BEAR
	1/31/2000	2.5218%	BULL	5/13/2009	-2.6895%	BEAR
	9/8/2015	2.5083%	BULL	9/9/2011	-2.6705%	BEAR

CHAPTER FORTY-THREE

Kirsner Wealth Management
<u>Team Biographies</u>

Craig Kirsner, MBA

**President of Kirsner Wealth Management and
Investment Adviser Representative
Author, Speaker, Forbes 2021 and 2002 Top
Financial Security Professional,**

Craig Kirsner, MBA, is an author, speaker, Forbes Magazine #179 Top 2021 Financial Security Professional and #26 Forbes Top 2022 Financial Security Professional in the entire State of Florida.[129] He is President of Kirsner Wealth Management whom you may have seen on Kiplinger, Forbes, CNBC, Fidelity.com, Nasdaq.com, Fortune, Reader's Digest, The South Florida Sun-Sentinel, US News & World Report, Yahoo Finance, HuffPost, MSN Money, Bankrate.com, and many others.[130] Craig was also featured on The Today Show discussing retirement strategies designed to help preserve your wealth and help minimize taxes.[131] Craig is the author of <u>Help Preserve Your Wealth and Leave a Legacy</u> and creator of the Help Preserve Retirement System.

Craig focuses on working with retirees who want to help preserve their wealth and leave a legacy to their family. The vast majority of his clients are retired and are now focusing on helping preserve their assets. Craig has a strategic partnership with estate planning attorneys to

---

[129] Forbes, 2022. "Craig Kirsner." https://www.forbes.com/profile/craig-kirsner/?list=financial-security-professionals/&sh=181a6a7422cc. Forbes Top Financial Security Professionals 2021 and 2022 is a ranking of financial professionals conducted by Forbes through the SHOOK evaluation process. To be considered by Forbes, Craig Kirsner was nominated by an insurance carrier he sells annuities through. Financial Security Professional (FSP) refers to professionals who are properly licensed to sell life insurance & annuities. FSP may also hold other credentials & licenses which would allow them to offer investments and securities products through those licenses. References to security refer only to the benefits of insurance products, not to investments. Insurance products are backed by the financial strength & claims paying ability of the issuing carrier. For more information on the FSP Ranking visit these links: https://www.forbes.com/sites/rjshook/2021/10/19/methodologyam ericas-top-ranked-financial-security-professionals2021/?sh= 55aab7e15fa9 & https://www.forbes.com/best-in-state-financial-security-professionals/?sh= 71ffb8c07f33#1f0adc5d18a8

[130] Media outlets do not recommend or endorse the author or the content of this book.

[131] Media outlets do not recommend or endorse the author or the content of this book.

help ensure that his clients' legal documents will work to accomplish their goals which typically include helping protect assets left to children from potential divorces and lawsuits, and helping keep assets in the family bloodline.

He is committed to every part of his clients plans being reviewed, attended to, cleaned up, completed, and kept up-to-date. His direct, "hands on" approach helps retirees wade through all the tough planning decisions. Craig is committed to his clients by making sure their plan is completed in a timely manner.

Craig and his staff are completely independent. They have long-term affiliations and experience with dozens of life insurance companies in the United States. Craig is a member of the Million Dollar Round Table (MDRT) and is part of the Top of the Table level, which includes some of the top insurance professionals in the industry by production. [132]

He has undergraduate degrees in Finance and Risk Management from the University of Florida, as well as an MBA in Finance from the Chapman School of Business at Florida International University. He has passed the Series 63 and 65 securities exams and has been a licensed life insurance agent since 1994. Craig learned from his dad, Stuart Kirsner, who started our business in 1972. Craig's book in late 2005 predicted the collapse of the real estate

---

[132] Million Dollar Round Table ("MDRT") is a membership organization. Qualifying criteria for membership include attaining specified levels of commissions earned, premium paid or income earned on the sale of insurance and other financial products. The MDRT membership requires the payment of annual dues, compliance with ethical standards, and to be in good standing with an MDRT-approved Professional Association. There are 3 levels of membership which include standard membership, Court of the Table and Top of the Table. The MDRT logo and/or trademarks are property of their respective owners and no endorsement of Craig Kirsner or Kirsner Wealth Management is stated or implied..

market and the subsequent recession and stock market crash.

Craig is a member of the following academic honor societies: Delta Epsilon Iota Academic Honor Society, Beta Gamma Sigma Business Honor Society, Phi Eta Sigma National Honor Society and Alpha Lambda Delta National Academic Honor Society.

He is married to Karen, and they have two sons Samuel and Adam. Karen and Craig have an English Bulldog and two Havanese dogs. He is active in a number of charities in the area. In 2007 he was awarded the Presidential Volunteer Service Award and in 2006 he was awarded "Volunteer of the Year" by Hands On Miami.

Sean Burke, M.S.

Vice-President of Kirsner Wealth Management and Investment Advisor Representative

Sean Burke, M.S., has his Master's degree in Financial Valuation and Investment Management. Sean has been seen on Forbes, Money, Kiplinger, Fidelity, Yahoo Finance, Bankrate.com, Nasdaq, U.S. News & World Report, MSN, Business Insider and more.

Sean's experience allows him to set up investment strategies that include tax-efficient investing with appropriate levels of risk management to help preserve principal. Sean was formerly with Fidelity where he was an Investment Consultant and Financial Adviser. Sean's article "Investment Strategies for the 4 Stages of the Economic Cycle" was seen on Kiplinger and Yahoo Finance.

Prior to joining our team, Sean was a Financial Advisor and Investment Consultant at Fidelity where he worked with clients and families to establish plans and strategies that help to achieve client's financial goals. These conversations include tax-efficient investing, investment strategy with proper risk management, estate planning, helping preserve principal and income, and more.

Sean is a scratch golfer who played competitively in college at Lynn University in Boca Raton. He is engaged to Brooke and has a Golden Retriever named Woods. Sean also enjoys spending time on the water, reading, and spending quality time with friends and family.

Chabelie Marte
Operations Manager & Director of Client Relations

Chabelie Marte graduated Magna Cum Laude from FAU in Early Care and Education and has over 7 years experience in child development. Chabelie is a passionate individual who enjoys getting to meet new people and exploring new places. She has a charismatic, compassionate, and loving personality, which is perfect for creating a warm, welcoming environment in our Coconut Creek office and to run the day to day operations of the company as Operations Manager.

Chabelie is married to Paul and they love animals and taking their chow/husky on long walks. She is of Dominican decent and was born in Long Island, New York, but loves the Florida heat.

Brianna Shepard
Director of Client Operations

Brianna is our accomplished Director of Client Operations who helps make sure all aspects of the back-office support needs are implemented properly. She is always striving for excellence in everything she does with a focus on delivering exceptional client service and ensuring client satisfaction. Born and raised in Boca Raton, Florida, she attended Florida Atlantic University and received her degree in both Sociology and Psychology.

Brianna loves to travel and try new restaurants, always seeking out new experiences and adventures. For her ideal weekend, she enjoys spending time with friends and family fishing in the Florida Keys.

Janae Jacobs
Client Operations Manager

Janae is 100% accountable that our clients' applications are done correctly and completed as quickly as possible... which she excels at. She takes great care of serving our client's needs. Janae spent 4 years completely running a chiropractic firm with 5 offices as their manager and public relations director.

Janae is also actively involved in giving back to the community. She volunteers at homeless shelters every year during the holidays, spreading joy and making the holiday season brighter for those less fortunate.

Alexis Lazo New Business Administrator

Alexis is our new Business Administrator who makes sure that all our client's applications are done accurately and properly.

Alexis graduated from Mary Baldwin University in 2019, where she majored in biology with a minor in anthropology. Alexis was inducted into the Miami High Hall of Fame for her outstanding achievements.

Prior to her current role, she worked as a Chiropractor's Assistant. Her passion and eagerness to take on new challenges make her an essential addition to our team.

Dallana Garcia Administrative Assistant

Dalia has her Masters in psychology from Rafael Urdaneta University in Venezuela. She was a practicing psychologist in Venezuela and worked with children for 11 years.

She moved to Florida in 2015 due to the political situation in Venezuela. Dalia is married with 1 son and loves to cook, read, travel and exercise.

CHAPTER FORTY-FOUR

Featured Appearances

Craig Kirsner, MBA, is an author, speaker, Retirement Planning Professional and Investment Adviser Representative whom you might have seen quoted on the following publications:[133]

Craig was seen on <u>The Today Show</u> discussing strategies designed to Help Preserve Your Wealth and Help Minimize Taxes.[134]

---

[133] Any media logos and/or trademarks contained herein are the property of their respective owners and no endorsement by those owners of Craig Kirsner or Kirsner Wealth Management is stated or applied. Media appearances were obtained through a PR program. The media outlets were not compensated in any way.

[134] The Today Show. Nov. 2, 2022. "New Rules for Retirement" https://www.today.com/video/retirement-checklist-how-to-plan-ahead-amid-rising-inflation-152271429588

Craig was on NBC 6 Miami News on January 17th, 2022 discussing How to Avoid Delays This Upcoming Tax Season[135]

Forbes "Obviously a year ago people were scared," says Craig Kirsner. "**The economy was shut down, the S&P was down 31% and the Dow was down 41% in only a 6-week period! People were having flashbacks to the 2008/2009 crash and were really getting concerned!**"[136]

Kiplinger **Retirees: Go Ahead and Spend More in the Go-Go Years:**

---

[135] Sasha Jones. NBC 6 Miami. January 17th, 2022. "Avoiding Delays This Upcoming Tax Season" https://www.nbcmiami.com/responds/avoiding-delays-this-upcoming-tax-season/2662941/

[136] Chris Carosa. Forbes. April 3, 2021. "How The Pandemic Actually Increased Financial Literacy." https://www.forbes.com/sites/chriscarosa/2021/04/03/how-the-pandemic-actually-increased-financial-literacy/?sh=597f58445559

The Go-Go Years (age 65 to 75) is a decade to focus on family, friends, travel, hobbies and anything else on the bucket list that requires an active lifestyle.

The Slower-Go Years (age 76 to 85) will be different. They may still be "go" years, but they will likely be slower-go years in many respects.

The Won't-Go Years (age 86 to 100) are a time when it may be more difficult to sustain as active a lifestyle as in the prior two decades."[137]

 "It's important for parents to talk to their adult children about money so that it gives them the knowledge to make better financial decisions," Craig Kirsner, president of Kirsner Wealth Management in Coconut Creek, Florida, says. [138]

Bankrate "The Probate process can take as long as one or two years to complete," says Craig Kirsner, president of Kirsner Wealth Management. "Court fees of up to 5% of your estate could be paid from the estate."[139]

---

[137] Craig Kirsner. Kiplinger. February 25, 2022. "Retirees: Go Ahead and Spend More in the Go-Go Years."
https://www.kiplinger.com/article/retirement/t062-c032-s014-retirees-go-ahead-and-spend-more-in-go-go-years.html
[138] Beth Braverman. U.S. News & World Report. June 6th, 2023. "How to Talk About Money With Family – and Why It's Important."
https://money.usnews.com/money/personal-finance/family-finance/articles/how-to-talk-about-money-with-family-and-why-its-important
[139] James Royal. Bankrate. June 21, 2022. "Revocable trust vs. will: A guide to estate planning in the age of coronavirus."
https://www.bankrate.com/retirement/revocable-trust-vs-will-estate-planning-coronavirus/

Craig was on NBC 6 Miami News on March 1st, 2023 discussing 5 Tips to Save Money Despite Inflation [140]

GO BankingRates

FORTUNE

Aol.

Rule No. 10 - Stay in the game, have an emergency fund "Keep 5 percent of your assets in cash, because challenges happen in life," says Craig Kirsner, president of retirement planning services at Kirsner Wealth Management in Pompano Beach, Florida. He adds: "It makes sense to have at least six months of expenses in your savings account."[141]

---

[140] Kris Anderson. NBC 6 Miami. March 1st, 2023. "Are You Living Paycheck to Paycheck? Here's 5 Tips to Save Money Despite Inflation" https://www.nbcmiami.com/news/local/are-you-living-paycheck-to-paycheck-heres-5-tips-to-save-money-despite-inflation/2983985/

[141] James Royal. Bankrate. January 5th, 2023. "The 10 golden rules of investing" https://www.bankrate.com/investing/golden-rules-of-investing/

SOUTH FLORIDA
SunSentinel
If you're afraid that you haven't put enough away for retirement, you're not alone. A recent study by the National Institute on Retirement Security found that 57% of working-age U.S. residents have no retirement savings at all. Only 28% of American workers feel confident that they will have enough money saved to retire comfortably.

Despite these conditions, there are still plenty of ways to properly plan for post-working life, says Craig Kirsner, president of and an investment advisor representative at Kirsner Wealth Management in Coconut Creek, Florida. [142]

YAHOO
FINANCE
Channel 9 went to an expert to find out what you should do first if you are the lucky winner of the lottery. One said to hold on to that money if you get it. "First thing you should do is absolutely nothing," said Craig Kirsner. "First thing, go out and get an amazing CPA and tax accountant so that before you even go in and claim your winnings, you're prepared." [143]

---

[142] Craig Kirsner. SunSentinel. May 18th, 2023. "Planning for retirement ahead of the next recession: 6 ways to do it"
https://www.sun-sentinel.com/sponsor-content-article/?prx_t=F2kIAQNVeA50QQA&ntv_acpl=1066215&ntv_acsc=0&ntv_ot=0&ntv_ui=344a6b92-e625-49a9-9b2b-9c715c4dcd77&ntv_ht=Ye1sZAA&fbclid=IwAR1loEvVBzsT8Pb-rj_Z_wj-kaeWFF-kXpD_XT_1YE3uUJJ8LZKGNy2tum4

[143] Phylicia Ashley,Adam Poulisse. Yahoo. July 29th, 2022. "If I had a billion dollars: What experts say you should do first if you win the Mega Millions"
https://news.yahoo.com/had-billion-dollars-experts-first-220232883.html

Kiplinger

Preparing for the Next Recession: Six Considerations for Retirees

1) How much risk do you want to take in your retirement plan, and how much do you have right now?

2) How much are you paying in fees in your retirement plan?

3) Help minimize your taxes!

4) Cut your expenses in retirement.

5) Make sure you're protected during retirement at the right price.

6) Consider modernizing your estate plan with an estate planning attorney.[144]

Craig was on CBS News Miami on August 25th, 2022 discussing Student Loan Forgiveness[145]

---

[144] Craig Kirsner. Kiplinger. May 11th, 2023. "Preparing for the Next Recession: Six Considerations for Retirees"
https://www.kiplinger.com/investing/prepare-for-next-recession-considerations-for-retirees

[145] Jacqueline Quynh. CBS News Miami. August 25th, 2022. "
Locals squeezed by skyrocketing rent say student loan forgiveness is a life changer"
https://www.cbsnews.com/miami/video/locals-squeezed-by-skyrocketing-rent-say-student-loan-forgiveness-is-a-life-changer/#x

Forbes "Most of our clients are the 'Millionaire Next Door' Baby-Boomers or older retirees ages 65 to 90," says Coconut Creek-based financial author Craig Kirsner. "This demographic is usually looking for something to help secure their wealth in, so when someone shows them a supposedly 'risk-free, no fee' magic solution, they see an answer to their prayers without actually knowing what they are buying."[146]

NASDAQ How Might Archegos' $10 Billion in Losses Affect Your Retirement? **Could derivatives cause the next financial crisis like they did in 2008?** In 2021, non-regulated Archegos caused over $10 billion in losses. Archegos was set up as a family office, away from the oversight of the SEC. As such they were allowed to take tremendous bets by using a derivative called a swap, which were bets on stocks using high leverage. Unfortunately, when those stocks went down, massive losses ensued. **It is believed that Archegos had $10 billion in assets, yet was allowed to bet on $50 billion to $100 billion of stocks! 5 to 10 times leverage spread out among a number of banks that took losses during March of 2021.** [147]

---

146 Chris Carosa. Forbes. December 31st, 2022. "DOL Warns Retirees: Watch Your Assets!" https://www.forbes.com/sites/chriscarosa/2022/12/31/dol-warns-retirees-watch-your-assets/?sh=3a8b41e17900

147 Craig Kirsner. Nasdaq. April 29, 2021. "How Might Archegos' $10 Billion in Losses Affect Your Retirement?" https://www.nasdaq.com/articles/how-might-archegos-%2410-billion-in-losses-affect-your-retirement-2021-04-29

WASHINGTON, D.C.

103.5 FM
WTOP.COM

You can elect to have your retirement savings withheld from your paychecks so you are not tempted to spend it now. "It's critically important to invest at least 10% of your current income for the future," says Craig Kirsner, president of retirement planning services at Kirsner Wealth Management in Coconut Creek, Florida. "Over time that has the potential to grow substantially with the power of compound interest." [148]

Kiplinger

Financial Advice for Millionaires: 5 Strategies for 2022
How millionaires can potentially save a lot in taxes and how to help protect the assets you leave your family and help keep them in your family bloodline long after you're gone.[149]

Reader's Digest

The US Post Office has been doomed to fail for some time, according to Craig Kirsner. One major problem is that the USPS is a quasi-government entity, so they have to be efficient like any company, while also having to pander to politicians who don't want their local post offices to close in order to protect the branch's employees' jobs (and the politicians'

---

[148] WTOP. October 24th, 2022. "How to Start Investing and Saving for Retirement With Little Money"
https://wtop.com/news/2022/10/how-to-start-investing-and-saving-for-retirement-with-little-money/

[149] Craig Kirsner. Kiplinger. February 7th, 2022. "Financial Advice for Millionaires: 5 Strategies for 2022"
https://www.kiplinger.com/retirement/604177/financial-advice-for-millionaires-5-strategies-for-2022

votes). "So even though from a business standpoint, it makes economic sense to close certain offices and consolidate things, they can't due to political pressure," he tells Reader's Digest. [150]

Forbes

Concerned about potentially higher taxes in the future?

Our U.S. government currently has over $29 trillion in debt, so you may be concerned about potentially higher income taxes in the future. If you have a substantial IRA (individual retirement account) accumulation, that could be a "ticking tax time bomb" that someone is going to pay taxes on in the future, whether it's you or your children after you're gone. [151]

Kiplinger

Most of our retired clients remember back when Internet access started with that annoying screeching sound when you dialed in over your phone line. Since then, we've seen the Internet transform by leaps and bounds. But get ready, because the Internet as we know it is on the cusp of making a quantum leap. And that could

---

[150] Elizabeth Yuko. Reader's Digest. Aug. 19, 2020. "What Could Happen if the U.S. Postal Service Stopped Delivering Mail?" https://www.rd.com/article/what-if-the-postal-service-stopped-delivering-mail/

[151] Craig Kirsner. Forbes. December 17th, 2021. "How Millionaires Can Potentially Save A Lot In Taxes And How To Help Protect The Assets You Leave Your Family And Help Keep Them In Your Family Bloodline Long After You're Gone" https://www.forbes.com/sites/forbes-shook/2021/12/17/how-millionaires-can-potentially-save-a-lot-in-taxes-and-how-to-help-protect-the-assets-you-leave-your-family-and-help-keep-them-in-your-family-bloodline-long-after-youre-gone/?sh=c10bc8c100b1

have a big effect on our pocketbooks and our lifestyles within the next few years. 152

Craig was on NBC 6 Miami News on April 8th, 2022 discussing How Federal Student Loan Debt Payments Are Paused Through August of 2022 153

YAHOO!
FINANCE
Some retirees start a new business or side hustle to continue to earn income after leaving their 9-to-5. In some cases, this can be a smart money move, but in others, it can be costly."This is, unfortunately, one of the biggest potential drains on a retiree's finances," said Craig Kirsner, MBA, author, speaker and president at Kirsner Wealth Management "The fact is that most businesses fail,

---

152 Craig Kirsner. Kiplinger. April 13th, 2022. "The Metaverse Explained (and Why You Should Care)"
https://www.kiplinger.com/investing/cryptocurrency/604532/the-metaverse-explained-and-why-you-should-care

153 Alina Machado. NBC 6 Miami. April 8th, 2022. "Federal Student Loan Debt Payments Paused Through August"
https://www.nbcmiami.com/news/local/federal-student-loan-debt-payments-paused-through-august/2732580/

so starting one in retirement is typically not a good idea, no matter how good the business idea sounds." [154]

GO BankingRates Forty-three% of super savers said they have driven older vehicles to save for retirement. **After the first 12 months of ownership, you can lose more than 20% of the car's value due to depreciation.** "[155]

Forbes Small businesses should be given priority in the Paycheck Protection Program (PPP). **"It was very unfortunate that the first PPP program allowed companies to receive up to $10 million. How does that qualify as a small business?** Biden should dedicate new PPP loans to businesses with 50 employees or less, true small businesses, and allow for more generous loans to allow businesses to cover capital costs and employee costs. [The government] should also put special focus on women and minority-owned businesses who have been hit especially hard during the Covid crisis," Kirsner said.[156]

---

[154] Jaime Catmull. Yahoo. May 8th, 2023. "29 Careless Ways Retirees Waste Money"
https://www.yahoo.com/lifestyle/29-careless-ways-retirees-waste-160001427.html?guccounter=1

[155] Gabrielle Olya. GoBankingRates. August 6, 2021. "19 Things You'll Need To Sacrifice Now for a Healthy Retirement."
https://www.gobankingrates.com/retirement/planning/things-to-sacrifice-now-for-healthy-retirement/

[156] Edward Segal. Forbes. Jan. 24, 2021. "What Many Small Businesses Need From Biden To Survive —And Recover—From The Covid Crisis."
https://www.forbes.com/sites/edwardsegal/2021/01/24/what-small-businesses-really-need-to-survive--and-recover-from-the-covid-crisis/?sh=70d0c0dd3608

"Higher interest rates are not good for a debt-fueled bubble like we're in now. Our economy is supported by tons of debt. Historically speaking, rising interest rates are typically the pin that pricks debt-fueled bubbles like we're in now, so the market is even more concerned that a recession could be coming.".[157]

"Having hobbies in retirement is so important for keeping both your mind and body busy. You've probably worked for decades and now you have to keep busy in retirement as well."[158]

[157] Ariel Zilber. New York Post. June 16, 2022. "Dow closes below 30,000 for first time since January 2021."
https://nypost.com/2022/06/16/dow-futures-fall-500-points-after-feds-sharp-rate-hike/amp/

[158] Brian O'Connell. U.S. News & World Report. September 20, 2022. "8 Great Hobbies in Retirement."
https://money.usnews.com/money/retirement/aging/articles/great-hobbies-in-retirement

Sean Burke, M.S. is a Retirement Planning Professional and Investment Adviser Representative whom you might have seen quoted on the following publications:[159]

Investment Strategies for the 4 Stages of the Economic Cycle

By Sean Burke, Investment Adviser Representative

The U.S. economy is cyclical in nature, surging ahead and pulling back in waves over time. Investors' portfolios need to change with the rise and the fall of that economic tide. Our goal is to manage the portfolio to find the highest potential rate of return for the least amount of risk (also known as risk-adjusted returns), adding growth potential during growth periods and adding principal protection through the use of insurance products, in times of uncertainty.[160]

---

[159] Any media logos and/or trademarks contained herein are the property of their respective owners and no endorsement by those owners of Craig Kirsner or Kirsner Wealth Management is stated or applied. Media appearances were obtained through a PR program. The media outlets were not compensated in any way.

[160] Sean Burke. Kiplinger. September 19, 2021. "Investment Strategies for the 4 Stages of the Economic Cycle." https://www.kiplinger.com/investing/603457/investment-strategies-for-the-4-stages-of-the-economic-cycle

"Bank collapses can affect the overall market performance," says Sean Burke, vice president and investment advisor representative at Kirsner Wealth Management in Coconut Creek, Florida. "It is important to diversify your portfolio which helps to spread risk over different asset classes and market sectors to avoid having too much risk in one sector of the market."[161]

Forbes

One other ETF worth consideration is Schwab U.S. Dividend Equity, which is designed to track as much as possible, before fees and expenses, the total return of the Dow Jones U.S. Dividend 100 Index. "We use it in most of our managed portfolios as it's a large cap, value stock ETF. It currently has a very nice 3.4% dividend yield," "It currently has a very nice 3.39% dividend payout. It has extremely low expenses of 0.06% per year."[162]

---

[161] Rachel Hartman. U.S. News & World Report. March 27, 2023. "Are 401(k)s Protected in a Bank Collapse?."
https://money.usnews.com/money/retirement/articles/are-401ks-protected-in-a-bank-collapse

[162] Erik Sherman. Forbes. May 22, 2023. "Best Dividend Stocks To Beat Inflation In 2023."
https://www.forbes.com/sites/investor-hub/article/best-dividend-stocks-to-beat-inflation/?sh=67dd8b9978ac

 "Parents who don't involve their children in financial discussions may be missing an opportunity to teach valuable lessons about money management and responsible financial behavior," You don't need to get into the nitty gritty of your finances with your children but explaining your financial philosophy or spending priorities – and why their request doesn't fit in – can help kids begin to think critically about how to spend money.[163]

And more!

If you'd like to find out how much risk you have now and how much you're paying in fees, join us for a dinner workshop at Ruth's Chris Boca Raton or Fort Lauderdale or Abe & Louie's in Boca Raton. Or meet

with Craig Kirsner, MBA, by calling 1-800-807-5558 or visiting www.KirsnerWealth.com.

---

[163] Maryalene LaPonsie. U.S. News & World Report. May 23, 2023. "10 Money Mistakes Parents Make." https://money.usnews.com/money/personal-finance/family-finance/slideshows/9-money-mistakes-parents-make

Kirsner Wealth Management

5350 West Hillsboro Blvd, Suite 103
Coconut Creek, Florida 33073
1-800-807-5558

www.KirsnerWealth.com
1-800-807-5558